ENGLISH EXPERIENCES

Susan Briggs

English Experiences

Written by Susan Briggs
Edited by Lesley Gilmour
Design by Metro

Published in 2003 by
Metro Publications
PO Box 6336
London
N1 6PY

Printed and bound in Spain by Imago

© 2003 Susan Briggs
British Library Cataloguing in Publication Data.
A catalogue record for this book is available from the British Library.

ISBN 1 902910 16 8

"Such books as make us happy, we could, if need be, write ourselves"

Franz Kafka

Acknowledgments

My strongest childhood memories are a combination of the excitement of exploration and discovering new places through books. My curiosity still spurs me on to find out more, to travel around and find new places and meet unusual people. This book wouldn't have been written without my parents feeding that curiosity and stimulating such a strong interest in the world around me. Nor without Elias and Nina as fellow explorers to check out some of the places mentioned.

This book also needed concrete information, mostly provided by 15 years in the tourism industry but also amply supplied by the press officers of the British Tourist Authority. For years I've been squirreling away piles of their press releases and media briefings – thank you.

Many thanks to my father Malcolm Briggs for taking so many of the photographs for this book and to the other photographers/contributors who supplied photos.

To Nina, hoping her dreams and travels always take her in the direction she wants to go and that she comes home safely.

CONTENTS

INTRODUCTION

FINDING THE ENGLAND OF YOUR IMAGINATION

If you're looking for "official" and completely unbiased information this book isn't for you. If you like the comfort zone of heavily branded hotels and standardised fast food outlets, you're unlikely to appreciate this book. It's aimed at both visitors to England and natives who want to enjoy England, visit places that aren't always obvious and to find new experiences.

This book contains an assortment of ideas and suggestions for the independent traveller. Some of the recommendations are personal, others are from friends and colleagues and others have been unearthed through my work in the tourist industry.

This book isn't intended to be comprehensive – it doesn't go into laborious detail about train services or how to find a camp-site because plenty of guidebooks do that. It simply aims to offer an insight and some inspiration for your next trip around England, whether it's an afternoon excursion with Auntie Nellie or a fortnight's in-depth exploration.

All over the world people are able to picture England in their mind's eye. A green, beautiful landscape with eccentric personalities, quaint cottages, and quirky places to visit. Centuries of history, inhabitants with an island mentality who eat peculiar food like puddings together with meat.

When they get the chance to visit England, they usually head for London. Some will venture outside the Capital to Scotland (for many overseas visitors this is also "England") or honey-pot destinations such as the Cotswolds. But these visitors remain just visitors. They may never discover the England they've pictured so clearly. They mostly see exactly the same sights as other tourists and see them surrounded by fellow tourists. The England of their imagination remains illusive, picture-book villages, eccentric characters in local pubs, living in old houses. They crave "insider tips" so they ask English people where to go and what to see...

And what of the English? Most of us also have a picture of the England we want to see, often dating back to cosy childhood days. And yet when overseas visitors ask us for "insiders' tips" we're stumped. We're often even secretly ashamed when overseas visitors have seen more of our country than we have.

Whether you're from England or overseas this book will help you to really experience the best of England, avoiding the mundane, escaping the corporate chains and seeking out the essence of "Englishness".

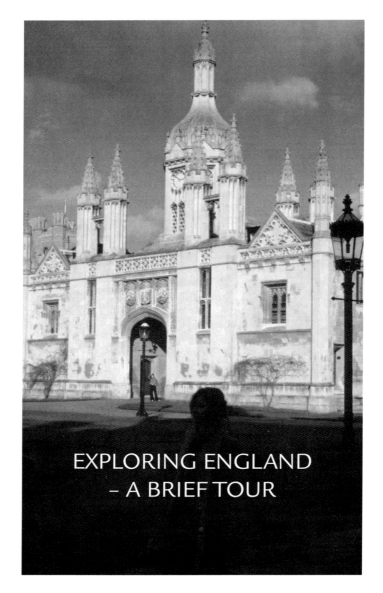

EXPLORING ENGLAND
– A BRIEF TOUR

WHAT TO SEE – KEY CITIES

When visiting a new country most of us make the capital city our first destination, basing our opinions of the country on an all too brief insight into its capital city. And yet, most capital cities are much larger, grander and altogether different from every other town in that country. London is ancient, modern, cosmopolitan, traditional, beautiful and ugly all at once. It's also completely unrepresentative of the rest of England. It has a vast range of new and historical attractions, and an overwhelming choice of places to eat, shop or stay. It's impossible to feel you really know every aspect of London, whereas most other towns and cities can be explored in a weekend.

For those who want to see as much as possible and take the "highlights" tour, this quick dash around England lists some of the main features of key cities and what to look out for. The following chapters will help you to explore in more depth and suggest other less obvious ways of really experiencing and enjoying England.

Bath is now a World Heritage Site because of the importance of its extensive Roman remains and fine Georgian architecture. Don't miss the Roman Baths and Museum where you can see the underground mineral springs, hypocaust heating system and a series of baths.

The must-have refreshment in Bath is a secret recipe "Sally Lunn bun" at Sally Lunn's Refreshment House, set in the oldest house in the city. Visit the Royal Crescent and see the carefully ordered townhouses or go to the Museum of Costume, which presents the story of fashion over the last 400 years.

Birmingham used to be somewhere you passed through as quickly as possibly, usually getting lost in the complicated network of roads known as "Spaghetti Junction". It's now transformed itself and its canals into a much more attractive and lively city. Make sure you explore the canal side walkways and visit the Jewellery Quarter, home to over 100 jewellery designers and makers.

The Symphony Hall is the home of the acclaimed City of Birmingham Symphony Orchestra. Birmingham is a multi-cultural city and the place to eat a Balti curry, a dish of pan-fried meat and vegetables which is an Anglo-Indian creation.

Brighton is a coastal town but the sea is almost incidental since its focus is now more on its nightlife, antiques and the Royal Pavilion. This famous landmark was built in the 18th century by George, the Prince Regent who called Brighton "London by the Sea". Marvel at the opulence of the Royal Pavilion complete with Indian Mogul exterior and fantasy Chinese interiors, stroll down The Lanes and look for (often overpriced) antiques or party in one of Brighton's many bars and nightclubs.

Bristol still has a bustling harbour side but it's very changed from the one which led to its reputation as an important maritime city. The warehouses are still there but enjoying a new life as restaurants, bars and shops.

The new @Bristol complex includes a "wild walk" featuring tropical wildlife and fauna, a science centre and IMAX cinema. Many visitors also come to see the Arnolfini Contemporary Arts Centre and two famous ships. The SS Great Britain was the first iron steam-ship and is moored on Bristol's harbourside close to The Mathew, a replica of John Cabot's ship that sailed to America in 1497.

Cambridge is largely pedestrianised (except no-one explained this to the many cyclists who whiz by on their ancient bikes) so it's easy to walk around and enjoy one of the most beautiful city centres in England. Its centuries' old tradition of learning and discovery are continuing as it is now also a hive of high-tech industry.

Highlights include the Fitzwilliam Museum, the University Botanic Gardens, and of course a journey along the river Cam on a punt. If you choose the latter it's best to hire a "chauffeur" too so you can just sit and watch and not risk falling in the Cam. King's College is one of the biggest draws thanks to its beautiful architecture and the King's College Choir who sing in the fan-vaulted chapel.

Canterbury is a small and beautiful city, home to the Archbishop of Canterbury, head of the Church of England. Visitors come to see Canterbury Cathedral and St. Augustine's Abbey as well as the medieval centre with its tiny side streets such as Mercery Lane with overhanging houses, so close they almost touch.

The Canterbury Tales visitor attraction gives a quick, albeit superficial, insight into life in Chaucer's Middle Ages. If you use your own imagination you can probably build an equally good picture by walking along the city walls. To go even further back in time you can also visit the Roman Museum, built around the ruins of a Roman townhouse and its intricate mosaic pavement.

Chester is a beautiful, historic city and should be better known than it is. Encircled by a two mile ring of Roman and medieval walls, it has well-preserved examples of Georgian and Victorian architecture. Chester also has the oldest racecourse in the country and probably England's oldest shop front in the medieval two-tier galleries called the "Rows". The Rows now house stylish boutiques where footballers' wives love to go to spend their wealthy husbands' money.

Hull was mainly visited by people arriving and departing from the famous docks but is slowly developing into a town to be visited for its own sake. It is hoped that Sir Terry Farrell's dramatic new building, "The Deep" (described as a "submarium" to distinguish it from a mere aquarium) will do for Hull what Frank Gehry's Guggenheim did for Bilbao and put Hull on the visitor map.

Hull's other main attraction is Wilberforce House, birthplace of the famous abolitionist and now a museum telling the story of his struggle to end the slave trade. There are also two novel trails to follow – the intriguing Seven Sea trail, an alphabet of fish from Anchovy to Zander leading visitors through the historic Old Town and an Ale Trail which highlights some of Hull's architectural wonders in the shape of its many pubs.

Leeds is another northern town enjoying its new image. Although it is set on the edge of the beautiful Yorkshire Dales, the city itself lost some of its Victorian splendour until recent efforts were made to halt its decline. It has now turned the tables and once again become quite a "showy" city, proud of its expensive and fashionable shops and many nightclubs. Harvey Nichols opened their first "outpost" outside London here.

This is just one of the English northern cities where you can view the strange phenomenon of "purple legs". For some unexplained reason, no matter how cold the weather (including snow) night-clubbers never, ever wear a coat. You will see men in t-shirts and women in short skirts, no tights and very skimpy tops, clearly shivering so much their legs have turned purple but fashion is fashion…

Two of Leeds other more conventional attractions are the Royal Armouries Museum (featuring many of the weapons previously displayed in the Tower of London) and the sculpture in the Henry Moore Institute.

Liverpool is almost impossible to think of without mentioning, The Beatles. Not surprisingly the award-winning "Beatles Story" visitor attraction is popular. Liverpool's heyday was really much earlier, in the 18th century when its fortune was made as a transatlantic trading port. Many of Liverpool's municipal buildings bear testimony to this former wealth – but you often have to look up to appreciate them and see beyond some tatty shop fronts.

One way of seeing the sights is to take a river trip on the Mersey Ferry. Another is to go to the Albert Docks which have been completely renovated, using the old buildings for homes, shops and the Tate Liverpool, displaying modern art. Two other reasons to visit are the city's two cathedrals – the neo-gothic Liverpool Cathedral and the modern Metropolitan Cathedral.

Manchester has some similarities with Leeds – these two northern towns are rivals and try to outdo each other with the best shopping and trendiest bars and clubs. Most of Manchester's wealth came through its role as the world's major cotton-milling centre, so it has many examples of fine Victorian architecture. Look out for the bees symbolizing Manchester's industry hidden in the architecture of the Town Hall.

Manchester United fans will appreciate the chance to take a tour of Old Trafford's "Theatre of Dreams", perhaps followed by a Chinese meal in Britain's largest Chinatown.

Newcastle and neighbouring **Gateshead** (they are only separated by the River) are worth visiting as much to meet "Geordie" people as for any other reason. They are legendary for their sense of humour, zest for life and ability to party, perhaps explaining why the newly renovated Quayside area is buzzing with evening activity in its many bars and restaurants.

There are two other vast reasons for visiting Newcastle and Gateshead – the "Angel of the North" and the "Bridge". The Angel of the North was created by sculptor Antony Gormley and towers above the A1 motorway in Gateshead, marking the entry to Tyneside. It is 20 metres high and has a wing span of 54 metres. The newly opened Gateshead Millennium Bridge opens and closes like a gigantic eye and links Newcastle with Gateshead.

Oxford is famous for its "dreaming spires" and its quiet college courtyards. The best-known of the colleges is probably Christ Church which is also the largest. The Ashmolean is considered one of the world's greatest museums – admission is free to this incredible collection of art and archaeology. As well as browsing in the countless bookshops, you can punt on the Charnel river, one of the best ways of getting away from the crowds.

Portsmouth is one of England's greatest maritime cities and offers the best opportunity to learn more about life at sea and explore nautical history. It has the combined attractions of the Historic Dockyard which includes several sites to visit – the HMS Victory, HMS Warrior, the Mary Rose, the Royal Naval Museum and Action Stations. It is still a working port and where many of the Royal Navy's modern warships are docked – you can take a closer look with a harbour boat trip.

Stratford-upon-Avon is famous as the home of William Shakespeare and it does seem as if he is everywhere! As well as the Royal Shakespeare Company's productions at the two river-side theatres, there are five wonderfully well preserved houses with a Shakespeare connection including Mary Arden's Cottage (Shakespeare's mother) at nearby Wilmcote.

Stratford-upon-Avon is worth visiting even if you don't want to know more about Shakespeare since it is in a beautiful location and is a great base from which to explore the Cotswolds. Another nearby attraction is picture-book perfect Warwick Castle, set in Capability Brown-landscaped gardens.

York is one of England's "honey pot" destinations and it is easy to see why. Its history can be traced from Roman times although it is more famous for its medieval buildings and the Minster. York Minster is an important landmark and the largest medieval cathedral in Northern Europe, with some of the stained glass windows dating back to the 12th century.

A walk along the city wall is a must as it gives a different perspective and chance to escape the crowds who congregate in the narrow streets such as the "Shambles", where half-timbered houses overhang the cobbled lane. This is where you'll also find lots of quaint "Ye Olde Tea Shoppes" in which to rest and refresh. The Jorvik Viking Centre was one of the first of a new breed of visitor attractions where visitors travel in a "time capsule" to see a reconstruction of 10th century York which includes "businesses, backyards and even bedrooms".

WHAT TO SEE – COAST & COUNTRYSIDE

One of England's great advantages as a holiday and short break destination is that you can see plenty of places within a relatively short space of time and distance. Staying in one spot and exploring fewer places in more depth is probably more rewarding but if you like the idea of seeing the varied landscapes of different counties, here's a brief insight.

Scotland is well-known for its castles but you'll also find many in the border country of **Northumbria** where numerous skirmishes and major battles between the Scots and English took place. Bamburgh Castle is one of the most picturesque as it's situated right on the coast with views across to **Holy Island** and Lindisfarne.

The Northumbrian coastline is dramatic and unspoilt. It may not enjoy such warm weather as Mediterranean countries but the natural beauty is stunning. The small fishing village of **Craster** is famous for its "kippers" (smoked haddock) and nature-lovers will enjoy a boat trip from Seahouses to the **Farne Islands** where grey seals and birds abound.

Stretching from the coast across to **Cumbria** is Hadrian's Wall and the Northumberland National Park in which Kielder Water is the largest man-made lake in Northern Europe. The man who is now in charge of the wardens there was once the local boy who switched on the tap to flood and create Kielder Water.

Cumbria's **Lake District** is of course known for its lakes, of which the most famous is Windermere. There are three personalities most associated with this area. The romantic poet, William Wordsworth wrote the words which at one time every English school-boy and girl were required to memorize...

"I wander'd lonely as a cloud
That floats on high o'er vales and hills,
When all at once I saw a crowd,
A host, of golden daffodils;
Beside the lake, beneath the trees,
Fluttering and dancing in the breeze…"

Visitors now flock to Wordsworth's former homes at Dove Cottage and Rydal Mount. Another favoured destination is the childhood home at Hill Top of children's author, Beatrix Potter whose animal characters have comforted and entertained countless children around the world.

Visiting any of these places, it is easy to think the Lake District is over-crowded and full of souvenir shops but literally following in the footsteps of the Lake District's other famous personality will take you into some of the most beautiful and remote areas. With his books and descriptions of walks and wildlife Alfred Wainwright was responsible for helping many walkers escape the tourists and enjoy lesser known areas of the Lake District. His guides are a great resource for those wanting to explore the Lake District in more detail.

Just below the Lake District is the **Lancashire** coast which has two very different identities. Towns like Blackpool and Morecombe are brash and colourful, visited by families on day-trips in search of amusement arcades, the famous Blackpool Illuminations and its white-knuckle rides. **Southport** is more genteel and although in theory it's a seaside town, it's perfectly possible to go there when the tide is out and not see the sea at all. It has vast expanses of golden sand. Southport is also known for its extensive flower beds and municipal gardens as well as the annual flower show.

The **Yorkshire Moors and Dales** attract walkers, artists and others wanting to enjoy a slightly gentler terrain. The scenic North Yorkshire Moors Railway is an easy way to see the Moors, running from Pickering to Grosmont near Whitby. The countryside of the Yorkshire Dales is mostly soft and undulating and prettier than the nearby Peak District which is starker and more dramatic. The Dales were the setting for the James Herriott books and some of the villages seem caught in a gentle, lost age of neighbourliness and friendship. The ruins of Whitby Abbey, Jervaulx Abbey, Rievaulx Abbey, and Fountains Abbey feel absolutely timeless.

The **Peak District** is really two quite different areas – the Light and Dark Peaks. The Dark Peak is brooding and almost melancholic in its wild, windswept moors. The Light Peak is softer and the pretty setting for Haddon Hall and Chatsworth House. It's an area loved by walkers and climbers alike and where England's first National Park was established.

The **Cotswolds and Severn Valley** also offer gentle hills with hidden valleys, and distinctive medieval market towns and villages, made of the famous honey coloured Cotswold stone. These are the "chocolate box" villages, seen in so many travellers' photo albums.

The **East of England** is known for its flat countryside and low skies. Pockets of the area such as Cambridge and the Norfolk Broads attract many visitors but much of the area seems a sleepy backwater where time stands still. If you hire a boat you can enjoy around 300 miles of shallow waterways on the **Norfolk Broads**, and it's very easy to get away from the crowds.

Some of the Suffolk towns and villages such as **Lavenham** and **Kersey** look like those in a children's story book, painted in pastel colours and with higgledy-piggledy medieval houses. This area is also great for antique hunters or for those wanting to enjoy paddling in the sea around the soft coastline or watching birds in the reed beds.

In the **South East**, the counties of **Kent**, **Sussex** and **Surrey** are full of leafy lanes, historic houses, gardens and tiny unspoilt villages. You really feel that you can see the ghosts of pirates and smugglers in pretty coastal towns like ancient **Rye** and its easy to imagine Anne Boleyn in her childhood home at Hever Castle. There are plenty of beauty spots on the coast and the **Isle of Wight** is just a short ferry ride away.

The **West Country** spreads across several counties. Much of Wiltshire is designated as an Area of Outstanding Natural Beauty. It's a mystical place – where you are most likely to spot corn circles, white horses cut into the hillsides and prehistoric sites such as **Stonehenge** and **Avebury**. **Dorset** has extensive heathlands in the east and woodland in the west of the county, as well as a craggy coast. The quaint town of **Lyme Regis** is still famous for its fossils.

Devon and Somerset have rolling hills, thatched villages and patchwork fields – the epitome of rural England. Dairy farming is prevalent in this area and it's also a popular place for family holidays on a farm, recreating the cosy atmosphere of Enid Blyton's Famous Five books.

Moving down towards **Cornwall** are the wild open spaces and dramatic scenery of **Dartmoor**. Cornwall is a favourite holiday destination, known for its coastal resorts such as the artists' town, St. Ives, surfers' paradise Newquay and jumbled, picturesque town Polperro. Cornwall becomes very busy during the Summer but it is still possible to find small, almost deserted coves if you venture down the narrow winding roads away from main resorts.

More information about places to visit and where to stay from these web sites and tourist boards:

British Tourist Authority
www.visitbritain.com

North West England
www.visitnorthwest.com

Cornwall and Devon
www.cornwall-devon.com

Northumbria
www.visitnorthumbria.com

Dartmoor
www.dartmoor.co.uk

Peak District
www.peakdistrict-tourism.gov.uk

East of England – East Anglia
www.eastofenglandtouristboard.com

South West England
www.visitsouthwestengland.com

Hadrian's Wall
www.hadrians-wall.org

Southern England
www.visitsouthernengland.com

Heart of England
www.visitheartofengland.com

Suffolk
www.heritage-suffolk.org.uk

Isle of Wight
www.islandbreaks.co.uk

York
www.york-tourism.co.uk

Lake District & Cumbria
www.golakes.co.uk

Yorkshire
www.yorkshirevisitor.com

Norfolk
www.visitnorfolk.co.uk

Wiltshire
www.wiltshiretourism.co.uk

A ROOF OVER YOUR HEAD

Unless you are fortunate enough to have many houses or lots of rich relatives, you are likely to need somewhere to stay as you travel around England.

There's no shortage of comfortable and cheap accommodation such as branded chain hotels and lodges, but they can be soulless places with no character or sense of their locality. I recommend avoiding these in favour of a more personalised experience.

With some forward planning and inside knowledge, you can find a temporary home which not only offers excellent value for money but can also become an experience in itself.

Bed & Breakfast – Even For Horses

England is world-famous for its "Bed and Breakfasts". When done properly these are some of the very best places to stay as they are usually quite cheap, offer a chance to meet "real people" (as opposed to the scripted service of chain hotels), literally to "feel at home" and to eat a good hearty English breakfast. There are countless guides listing some of the best B&Bs but before you use one, do make sure its impartial and the recommendations are not driven by advertising. Some of the more reputable accommodation guides are listed at the end of this chapter.

People offering B&B come from all walks of life. Many of the countryside B&Bs are examples of the need for farmers to diversify and find alternative income so if you stay in farmhouse accommodation, you're helping to preserve a way of life and likely to enjoy home produce for breakfast. Farm Stay UK has over 900 farms offering B&B or holiday home accommodation. Most of them are still working farms, ideal touring centres, and generally offer excellent value for money.

Some B&B hosts living in grand houses are not as rich as their large residences might indicate. "Lloyds names" (people who invested heavily in the insurance institution but got caught out with bad risks) and even aristocrats suffering from the impact of death duties feel the need to let rooms and make money in an ever-so-genteel way. Other hosts do it because they enjoy the company or want to use rooms vacated by their offspring who have flown the family nest.

Apart from spotting B&Bs by their signs as you drive around the country, or using one of the guidebooks, you can get lists of B&Bs from Tourist Information Centres or turn to one of the many consortia. They don't directly own any of the B&Bs they represent but act as marketing agencies on behalf of the hosts. In fact one of the benefits of staying in a B&B is that they are all privately owned houses reflecting their owners' personalities, tastes and individual quirks.

Wolsey Lodges is a consortium of almost 200 privately-owned homes welcoming guests. Based on the idea of offering good quality B&B, the key difference is that their establishments also offer dinner and all bedrooms have a private bathroom so there is no need for midnight dashes down a cold corridor. Some of the houses are very grand. You might find yourself staying in a timber-framed Elizabethan house in Hertfordshire, a Regency villa in County Durham or a 300 year old Somerset mill. B&B prices in Wolsey Lodges range from £25-£70 per person per night, averaging around £37 so they compare favourably with hotels.

Other consortia and agencies specialise in different aspects of B&B. Garden enthusiasts can choose to stay with hosts who share their interest. 100 homes with beautiful gardens are promoted by "Bed and Breakfast for Garden Lovers" and usually cost around £30 per person per night. About half of the hosts are also willing to provide an evening meal and all of them will give recommendations for nearby restaurants or pubs serving food.

It seems there is a B&B to suit almost anyone – the British Horse Society publishes a great book called "Bed and Breakfast for Horses" featuring over 400 places in the UK which offer accommodation for horses and in many cases squeeze in space for their owners too...

"Uptown Reservations" have around 80 London homes on their books, mainly in Central London. Most of the homes are quite upmarket, full of character and very friendly. At around £40 per person per night including breakfast this is certainly a cheaper and more personalised option than most Central London hotels.

SOMETHING DIFFERENT...

If you're looking for a place to stay with plenty of character, the "Distinctly Different" consortium is definitely for you. It was started by a couple who offer bed and breakfast in their converted watermill in Bradford-on-Avon and whose guests constantly asked them if they knew of other "different" places in which to stay. They travelled around the country vetting other properties and rating them accordingly to their level of "differentness".

Now the consortium includes a converted double-decker bus sleeping eight people (which tours around Yorkshire), former lighthouses, wind and watermills, a Victorian railway station, 13th century manor house, chapel of rest, a court and police station and even a one-time boatman's brothel. Prices are very reasonable and start at just £17 per person per night, with the average around £35.

There are Distinctly Different properties around the country and they are an excellent way of finding out what it feels like to live inside a historic property. Distinctly Different is one of those "insider secrets" which everyone thinks twice about passing on but the word is getting about. These places are not just somewhere to stay for a night but homes you can really enjoy and tell your friends about. They are popular so make sure you book early.

HOMES WITH A HISTORY

If you're interested in historic and quirky buildings, The Landmark Trust directory is a must. The Landmark Trust's philosophy is simple – people staying in the properties pay towards their preservation by doing so and the Trust continues to restore "new" buildings to add to the collection. They already have over 80 properties in England which have been restored and made habitable, often from a parlous state. They include Bath Houses, Gatehouses, Mills, Mansions, Priories, Follies, and entire hamlets such as Coombe in Cornwall.

One of my most memorable English experiences was staying in a tiny cottage (actually it used to be a pigsty belonging to the lighthouse keeper) on Lundy Island, just off the coast of Devon. A ferry takes passengers over to the island which is just three miles long, has a population of about 18, three light-houses, a castle, campsite, church and numerous houses and cottages, mostly belonging to the Landmark Trust. Quite a lot of passengers just go for the day but if you can rent a Landmark Trust property on the island then you get the extra joy of standing watching from the cliff top as the afternoon ferry leaves the island and knowing you are truly marooned.

Anyone wanting to escape the daily grind of modern life is well advised to spend some time on Lundy. There's no television, an erratic power supply and only a tiny shop. Marisco Tavern is a meeting place for everyone staying on the island as well as a shelter in storms for those who've chosen to camp.

Landmark Trust prices are reasonable considering the experience which is on offer. They range enormously according to season and the size and relative comfort of the property – you can also snap up a last minute bargain, especially in the winter months. Don't be put off by bad weather, since many of the properties have roaring open fires, a good stock of books and cosy lounges.

A similar but smaller organisation is the Vivat Trust which is also dedicated to rescuing neglected buildings of architectural, historical or industrial interest. It has several properties including North Lees Hall, an Elizabethan tower house in the Peak District, Church Brow Cottage overlooking the River Lune at Kirkby Lonsdale in the Lake District and the Chantry in Bridport, Dorset dating from about 1300.

The National Trust also has over 300 cottages to let. There's a huge range from a 19th century miner's cottage for two people to a former farmhouse which accommodates 12. One of the advantages of many of the National Trust properties is that they are often in the grounds of grander places owned by the National Trust and in some of the most beautiful countryside in the country.

Anyone looking for a self-catering holiday with real style should take a look at the website for Luxury Cottages Direct which offers nothing but four and five star holiday homes in the form of cottages, farmhouses and apartments. Many of them have swimming pools and other touches of glamour.

STAY IN AN INN

In "olden times" travellers broke their long arduous journeys by staying at an inn. This is becoming a popular option again now as pub and inn landlords seek to diversify and extend the range of services on offer. Pub food is often excellent especially in the trendy "gastro pubs".

There is an alliance of independently-owned old inns called Great Inns of Britain which has about 16 members, all of which were invited to join after they had met exacting criteria regarding their bedrooms, service, character, ambience and food. Members include the 14th century Rising Sun at Lynmouth where Exmoor reaches the sea, the Boar's Head in North Yorkshire next to Ripley Castle (well worth a visit – ask the house-keeper to tell you about the tea hierarchy) and the Seaview on the Isle of Wight.

HOLIDAYS AFLOAT

You can combine accommodation with travel by enjoying a holiday afloat. England has an extensive network of waterways, rivers and canals so you can choose from traditional narrow boats or barges, motor cruisers, hotel boats and sailing craft. Details are available from Waterway Holidays UK, the national marketing company for inland waterways who have details of over 80 boat hire and hotel boat operators.

YOUTH HOSTELS – NOT JUST FOR THE YOUNG

Youth Hostels used to conjure up visions of draughty old places that only the young and adventurous would want to stay in. They've changed! As you walk through villages and countryside on some of England's best known routes such as the Pennine Way you'll notice that many of the large rambling old buildings have been converted into Youth Hostels with a warm welcome for people of all ages. Alongside young students, you're now as likely to find a group of active senior citizens or a family of six staying there.

Some of the buildings are truly stunning. You can stay in a log cabin, an isolated shepherd's cottage or even a moated Norman castle in Gloucestershire. There are now also far fewer dark cold corridors to wander through in search of a loo, since the Youth Hostel Association upgraded their facilities and installed many more bathrooms, some en-suite. They offer exceptional value for money with prices starting at around £7 per person per night.

Budget travellers will also appreciate a group of backpackers' hostels owned by St. Christopher's Inns which offers "safe, clean, fun and cheap" accommodation from £12 per person per night. They have several sites in London including one near London Bridge where you'll also find hot tubs, saunas and internet connections. It seems even budget accommodation is going upmarket!

Classification & Grading Systems

Whatever type of accommodation you choose, sooner or later you will come across the new classification system for hotels and guest accommodation. Until recently the English Tourism Council, AA and RAC all operated their own inspection and ratings schemes which was very confusing to the consumer, especially when the same hotel was rated differently by different organisations. In theory this is no longer a problem as the three agencies have joined forces to create one new overall rating scheme. Unfortunately there is a transition period so for some time to come it's likely that you'll still see some of the old ratings as well... But just so you're prepared here's what the new system of stars and diamonds mean.

Stars & Diamonds – what they mean

'★' **Stars** are used for hotels and '♦' **diamonds** for "guest accommodation" which means B&Bs, guesthouses, inns and farmhouses. There's a similar star ratings system for caravans and campsites. All accommodation using this system will have been visited by qualified, independent assessors.

Star and diamond ratings symbolize the level of service, range of facilities and quality of guest care that you can expect. Hotels are required to meet progressively higher standards as they move up the scale from One to Five Stars.

★

Means a limited range of facilities and services but a high standard of cleanliness. Friendly and helpful staff. Restaurant/eating area open to you and your guests for breakfast and dinner. A bar or lounge serving alcohol. 75% of bedrooms will have en-suite or private facilities.

★★

Means all the above plus more comfortable and better equipped bedrooms, – all with en-suite or private bathrooms and colour TV. A straightforward range of services, with a more personal touch. Food and drink is of a slightly higher standard. A lift is normally available.

★★★

Means all the above plus greater quality and a higher standard of facilities and services, and usually more spacious public areas and bedrooms. A more formal style of service, room service including continental breakfast. Laundry service available. Greater attention to quality of food.

★★★★

Means all the above plus superior comfort and quality; all bedrooms with en-suite bath, fitted overhead shower and WC. Spacious and very well appointed public areas with strong emphasis on food and drink. Skilled staff anticipating and responding to your needs and requests. Room service of all meals, 24 hour drinks, refreshments and snacks.

★★★★★

Means all the above plus spacious, luxurious establishment offering the highest international quality of accommodation, cuisine, services and a range of extra facilities, and services. Professional, attentive, highly trained staff. Striking décor, exceptional comfort and a sophisticated ambience.

♦

Means clean accommodation, providing acceptable comfort with functional decor and offering at least a full cooked or continental breakfast. Where other meals are provided they must be freshly cooked. Clean bed linen, towels and fresh soap. Adequate heating and hot water available at reasonable times for baths or showers at no extra charge. An acceptable overall level of quality and helpful service.

♦♦

Means all the above plus a higher level of quality and comfort with greater emphasis on guest care in all areas.

♦♦♦

Means all the above plus a good overall level of quality. Well maintained, practical decor; a good choice of quality items available for breakfast; other meals, where provided, will be freshly cooked from good quality ingredients. A good degree of comfort provided for you, with good levels of customer care.

♦♦♦♦

Means all the above plus a very good overall level of quality in all areas and customer care showing very good levels of attention to your needs.

♦♦♦♦♦

Means all the above plus an excellent overall level of quality. For example, ample space with a degree of luxury, an excellent quality bed, high quality furniture, excellent interior design. Breakfast offering a wide choice of high quality fresh ingredients; other meals, where provided, featuring fresh, seasonal local ingredients. Excellent levels of customer care, anticipating your needs.

More information about accommodation in England:

Bed & Breakfast for Garden Lovers
www.bbgl.co.uk

British Holiday & Home Parks Association
(self-catering accommodation eg in caravans and chalets)
www.bhhpa.org.uk
Tel: 01452 526911

British Horse Society
www.bhs.org.uk
Tel. 08701 202 244

Camping & Caravanning Club
(network of campsites)
www.campingandcaravanning-club.co.uk
Tel: 0204 7669 4335

Caravan Club (main organisation for touring caravanners with wide range of quality sites)
www.caravanclub.co.uk
Tel: 01342 326944

Distinctly Different
www.distinctlydifferent.co.uk
Tel: 01225 866842

Farm Stay UK
www.farmstayuk.co.uk
Tel: 024 7669 6909

Great Inns of Britain
www.greatinns.co.uk
Tel: 01432 770152

Landmark Trust
www.landmarktrust.co.uk
Tel: 01628 825925

Luxury Cottages Direct
www.findcottages.co.uk
Tel: 01454 324840

National Trust Cottages
www.nationaltrustcottages.co.uk
Tel: 0870 4584422

St. Christophers Inns
www.st-christophers.co.uk
Tel: 020 7407 1856

Uptown Reservations
www.uptownres.co.uk
Tel: 020 7351 3445

Vivat Trust
www.vivat.org.uk
Tel: 020 7930 8030

Waterways Holidays
(boat hire on inland waterways)
www.waterwayholidaysuk.com
Tel: 0870 241 5956

Wolsey Lodges
www.wolsey-lodges.com
Tel: 01473 822058

Youth Hostels Association
www.yha.org.uk
Tel: 0870 870 8808

ACCOMMODATION GUIDES

There are numerous accommodation guides available, some
more comprehensive than others and some more influenced by
their advertisers than independent inspectors.

The English Tourism Council is the national body for English
Tourism and the main organisation responsible for setting
accommodation standards. They publish a range of publications which are listed below. Each of the guides are updated
annually. You can order online *www.englishtourism.org.uk* or by
phone *0870 606 7204*.

Where to Stay: Bed & Breakfast Guest Accommodation
Includes guesthouses, bed & breakfast, farmhouses and inns.
Illustrated in full colour. Features the new national Diamond
ratings. Contains exclusive national list of all ETC quality-
assured guest accommodation.

Where to Stay: Hotel Accommodation
Guide to hotels, townhouses, travel accommodation. Illustrated
in full colour. Features the new national Star ratings. Contains
exclusive national list of all ETC quality-assured hotels.

Where to Stay: Self-Catering Holiday Homes
Guide to cottages, barns, houses, bungalows, flats, studios,
chalets and houseboats. Illustrated in full colour. Features the
national star ratings.

Where to Stay: Camping & Caravan Parks in Britain
Includes Holiday Parks, Touring Parks and Camping Sites.
Features the new national Star ratings.

Somewhere Special
Includes accommodation achieving the highest standards in
facilities and quality of service. Full colour presentation with
features, maps and places to visit.

Accessible Britain

First comprehensive official guide to accommodation for disabled people, including all establishments assessed under the National Accessible Scheme & showing a Tourist Board National Quality Rating.

RAC (www.rac.co.uk, tel: 08000 726 999)
AA (www.theaa.co.uk, tel: 01206 255 800)
The two main motoring organisations above, work in partnership with the English Tourism Council and also publish well-established accommodation guides, much of which can be consulted online.

RAC Hotels and Bed & Breakfast guide

Full colour guidebook to 3500 quality Hotels and B&Bs throughout the UK and Ireland, each one inspected and rated by RAC's team of inspectors. Hotels and Guest Accommodation for every taste and pocket – from five star luxury to cosy B&B's

AA Britain's Top Bed & Breakfast

Over 450 B&Bs offering the very best of British hospitality. All entries have been individually selected at the personal recommendation of AA inspectors from B&Bs in England, Scotland, Wales and Northern Ireland.

The AA Hotel Guide

Britain's best-selling hotel guide. Choose from over 4,000 hotels, many illustrated with a colour photograph, in England, Scotland, Wales, Ireland, Channel Islands and Isle of Man. Anonymous annual inspections from experienced AA inspectors ensure an accurate assessment of the accommodation.

TRANSPORTS OF DELIGHT

I've never quite understood the meaning of the saying "to travel hopefully is better than to arrive". Certainly in some cases the anticipation of arrival can be better than the actual event if the destination is a disappointment. For most of us though, we are pretty happy to get to our destination and the journey is just a necessary evil.

But if you're only taking a short break or even a day trip, it seems a pity to spend a couple of hours travelling and not enjoy the journey itself. Perhaps we should take a different approach, make travelling an integral part of our trip and actually plan to take pleasure in it? I'm not just talking about loading the car with story tapes, games and the kind of junk food you only permit yourself on long journeys, but suggesting you consider some "new" forms of transport. How about making the getting there part of the holiday itself?

Unusual Ways To Travel

You may use a conventional form of transport to get to your destination, but find alternative forms when travelling around once you get there. In Somerset, for example, you can enjoy the scenery of the Quantock Hills from the rather unusual vantage point of a friendly camel. In the Lake District, llamas can be on hand to carry your bags as you struggle up the hillsides.

Companies in the Lake District seem set on making it easier to enjoy the hills and dales. Mountain Goat is a long-established company which uses mini-buses to take visitors on scenic routes through the twisting passes and tiny roads to hidden beauty which are otherwise inaccessible to tourists travelling on bigger coaches.

Another option in the Lake District is to cycle but with such steep inclines that can be rather strenuous. A company called Easyriders aims to "take the puff out of pedalling" by hiring out environmentally friendly electric bicycles. They use a rechargeable battery and are silent running so particularly appropriate for quiet rural areas.

CYCLING – RECYCLED

Cycling is becoming increasingly popular, both as a leisure activity and a means of transport. Sustrans is a sustainable transport charity, working on practical projects to encourage people to walk, cycle and use public transport in order to reduce motor traffic and its adverse effects. The charity's flagship project is the National Cycle Network, creating 10,000 miles of routes throughout the UK.

There are already over 6,000 miles of continuous and safe cycle routes which reach all parts of the UK and the aim is that there will eventually be cycle paths passing within 2 miles of half the population.

About one-third of the current Network is on paths which are free from motor traffic, with the rest using quiet lanes or traffic-calmed roads in towns or cities. Traffic-free sections provide a suitable place for children and new cyclists to practice their skills. Many are also used by walkers, people with disabilities and in some cases, horse riders.

The National Cycle Network has tried to make the journey by bike more interesting and commissioned artworks to create distinctive landmarks and celebrate local characteristics. Some of these artworks are single pieces and others are part of a sequence which can be discovered over a longer distance. They also range in size from small discrete carvings to gigantic sculptures that you can spot from a distance.

Some are purely decorative, others are functional, providing drinking fountains, signs or seats along the way. Where-ever possible the artist responsible for the artwork has tried to respond to its specific site. By commissioning artworks, Sustrans hopes to encourage people to look more closely at the passing landscape (and to care about it) as well as making the journey enjoyable and interesting.

If you'd like to experiment with the idea of a cycling holiday by taking just a day trip to begin with or prefer to take the risk out of route planning, companies like Country Lanes offer organised day trips and very civilised cycling holidays in the Cotswolds, Lake District and New Forest using excellent accommodation in B&Bs or country house hotels. They even arrange delivery of your luggage each day so you don't have to carry it on your back.

Each of England's Regional Tourist Boards offers plenty of information about cycle routes but if this is your first cycling trip you might want to start in East Anglia where you're almost guaranteed no hills! There's a 370 mile National Cycle Network route from Hull to Harwich in the East of England which forms part of a 4,000 mile North Sea cycle route, linking England and Scotland and with the use of ferries connecting with cycle routes in Norway, Denmark, Germany and the Netherlands.

MESSING ABOUT ON THE WATER

East Anglia is also a popular destination for those who enjoy messing about on the water. Travelling by canal or river seems to be enjoying a renaissance thanks perhaps to various rounds of regeneration and lottery funding. We're now being encour-aged to use canals and inland waterways instead of roads. England's canal system was built over 200 years ago. The advent of the canals was similar to the early days of the dot-com revolution when people clamoured to invest. At their peak there were 4,250 miles of navigable rivers and canals carrying 30 million tonnes of freight a year.

Although some freight carrying continued until the early 1960's (when the motorways were built), the coming of the railways killed off most of this thriving canal network. Many canals were abandoned or even filled in. Just a couple of years ago, there was a realisation that the renovation of the inland waterways would be beneficial and more funding has been forthcoming for British Waterways to regenerate and re-build some of the canal network. 200 miles of waterway are now being re-opened so you can travel by boat or enjoy a different view by walking along the river paths. Many paths have areas suitable for cycling as well as being pushchair and wheelchair friendly.

Short sightseeing trips by boat are now available in destinations you might not associate with tourism – including the Sheffield canal featured in the film, "Full Monty". If you're interested in the story of the canals, the National Waterways Museum in Gloucester tells their story with special displays and events and The London Canal Museum in King's Cross is a great resource in the Capital.

Longer stays afloat are still popular. There's a plethora of boating and barge holidays on offer, using well-known water-ways like the Norfolk Broads as well as lesser known routes in the West Country and Black Country.

Barge holidays have long been popular but suddenly destinations like the Docklands in London are looking to hotel boats as the solution to an accommodation and land shortage. You'll soon be able to stay on a cruise ship, without getting sea sick. And for a river trip with a difference, why not try a trip in an amphibious vehicle that takes passengers on a tour by road and river through the heart of London with a "Frog Tour"?

STEAMING AHEAD

Back on dry land most of the train operating companies have some excellent offers to tempt passengers to travel by rail. It's a good option, especially during peak holiday times when the roads are likely to be busy.

Riding on a steam train adds a touch of novelty and nostalgia, and they often take scenic routes through some of England's most beautiful countryside. Probably the most famous and spectacular of all was the route through the Yorkshire Dales on the Settle – Carlisle Railway on which steam trains still run from time to time.

For those who are really interested in the age of the steam there's a new museum STEAM near Swindon. Several places around the country such as Severn Valley even offer the chance to drive and fire a real steam locomotive. To experience a really unusual railway in action you'll need to go to Lynmouth in North Devon and ride on the Lynton & Lynmouth Cliff Railway which is powered by an ingenious water system which does not involve steam.

FOUR LEGS GOOD

Another old-fashioned form of transport is still very popular in the UK, horse-riding. Horse-riding holidays are available for everyone from beginner to professional in all areas of the country. A national network of bridle-routes means you can avoid the traffic and confine your wanderings to leafy lanes.

There are even horse-friendly B&Bs (see page 19) for those who want to bring their own horse and plenty of horse-riding stables where you can hire a horse for anything from a one hour hack or several day trek.

Horses help to operate another unusual transport system on the Isle of Man where horse-drawn trams are still used on the seafront during the summer months.

And if this all seems too hectic for you there's still one option left. You can't be exactly certain where you'll head if you travel by hot air balloon but you are guaranteed some excellent views of the beautiful English countryside…

More information:

British Horse Society
www.bhs.org.uk
Tel: 08701 202244

Canal and Barge Holidays
www.britishwaterways.co.uk
Tel: 01923 201120

Country Lanes
www.countrylanes.co.uk
Tel: 01425 655022

Easyriders
www.easyriders.co.uk
Tel: 015394 32902

Frog Tours
www.frogtours.com
Tel: 020 7928 3132

Great Western Railway
www.steam-museum.org.uk
Tel: 01793 466646

Isle of Man
www.visitisleofman.com
Tel: 01624 686766

Mountain Goat
www.lakes-pages.co.uk
Tel: 01539 445161

National Waterways Museum
www.nwm.org.uk
Tel: 01452 318056

Settle – Carlisle Railway
www.settle-carlisle-
railway.org.uk

**STEAM – Museum of the
Severn Valley Railway**
www.svr.co.uk
Tel: 01299 403816

**Sustrans and the National
Cycle Network**
www.sustrans.org.uk
Tel: 0117 929 0888

**Information about other
transport not covered in
this chapter:**

The **RAC** and **AA** both have
excellent websites with route
planning facilities:
www.rac.co.uk
www.theaa.co.uk

National Express
(coach service)
www.gobycoach.com

Travel by Train
www.railtrack.co.uk
(for timetables & route planning)

www.qjump.co.uk
(to buy tickets online)

EAT, DRINK AND BE MERRY

There's no doubt about it. Food is fashionable. British attitudes towards food have changed hugely in the last ten years. No longer just something to be eaten before dashing off to enjoy more interesting pursuits, food has become more central to our thoughts and leisure time. The English are re-discovering their own food heritage and actually taking pride in it.

There are probably three dishes which overseas visitors most strongly associate with England: Roast Beef and Yorkshire Pudding; Fish and Chips (unfortunately no-longer wrapped solely in newspaper due to hygiene regulations); and the great English breakfast of bacon, eggs, sausages, mushrooms, fried bread, and tomatoes.

All of these are still eaten and enjoyed. Fashions change and for a time it was rare to see some old-fashioned stalwarts of British cuisine on restaurant menus. They turned instead to "nouvelle cuisine" and more recently to "modern British" and "fusion" food. But some of the old favourites are making an appearance on menus once again. These include toad-in-a-hole (sausages baked in the oven in a Yorkshire Pudding type batter), sausage and mash, and lots of delicious puddings like Jam Roly-Poly and Spotted Dick.

A GASTRONOMIC TOUR

Practically every area of England can contribute to a tour of the gastronomic pleasures. Northumbria has well-known delights such as Salmon from the River Tyne and Craster kippers as well as curious dishes such as "Singin Hinnies" and Stotty Bread which could perhaps be washed down with Newcastle Brown Ale. You're also likely to be offered Pan Haggerty, made from pan-fried layers of potatoes, onions and meat.

Yorkshire's most famous speciality is Yorkshire Pudding. Visitors from overseas inevitably find this an odd dish as it's eaten not as a dessert like other puddings but (in the case of true Yorkshire folk) as a starter. Yorkshire Pudding (made from flour, eggs and milk/water) is a sort of batter baked in the oven and usually moistened with gravy. It was traditionally given to the head of the household to fill him up when there was only a small amount of meat available. Luckily, such necessity is now a rarer reason for eating Yorkshire Pudding which is more frequently enjoyed as an accompaniment to roast meat, potatoes and vegetables.

We do seem to be a bit careless with the names of our cakes and puddings. Neither Kendal Mint Cake nor Black Pudding even vaguely resemble dessert-type pudding or cake. Kendal Mint Cakes are blocks of mint and sugar intended to fortify climbers and walkers in the Lake District but also eaten by anyone else with a particularly sweet tooth. Black Pudding is not quite so sweet – it's made from dried pig's blood and is more of a sausage than a pudding.

Argument continues to rage over whether Bakewell Tart is called Bakewell Tart or Pudding – there's also an ongoing debate in the Derbyshire town as to its origins and who makes it best but that's another story…

The Heart of England considers itself a gastronomic hot-spot. This is where you'll find Herefordshire Beef and Cider, the classic pig breeds of Staffordshire and Gloucestershire, and traditional cheeses such as Stilton and Double Gloucester. There are numerous small breweries in this region as well as it being the source of well-known mineral waters such as Buxton, Malvern and Ashbourne. Market Drayton is renowned for its Gingerbread which is supposed to possess aphrodisiac properties!

The Heart of England is also where you'll find some of England's best asparagus and the Melton Mowbray Pork Pie made with a "hand-raised" pastry within a day's horse ride of the town's market, and soon to receive Protection of Geographical Indication (PGI) status from the European Commission which is similar to the "Appellation Controllee" system used in France. A must for "Foodies" is Ludlow, described by John Benjamin as 'the loveliest town in England' and which now has three restaurants with Michelin stars (more than any other town outside the capital).

East Anglia gives us the interesting and potentially powerful combination of Norwich Mustard and Colchester oysters. It's also home to excellent apple juices, many real ale breweries and countless market gardeners.

The countryside of Suffolk in eastern England is well-known as the setting for beautiful Gainsborough and Constable paintings and is also the home of Suffolk ham, many fruit juices and a "Potato Tasting Festival". Giffords Hall run a potato festival in September, baking, chipping and mashing 25 different varieties of potato.

We call Kent the "Garden of England" but it's also famous for its distinctive oast-houses, which were used for drying hops ready to brew beer. Although most of these are no-longer in use, Kent still makes a major contribution to our drinks industry, through its wine as well as its beer.

The English wine industry is growing from strength to strength and we now have over 300 wine producers. Having flourished in Roman times, many of the vineyards in Southern England disappeared until after World War II. Don't make the mistake of thinking these are all relatively sweet white wines with little "bite". A growing number of English vineyards are now producing sparkling white wine as well as full bodied red

wine. You can visit around 100 of the vineyards and sample their range in Kent.

Also in the South of England, Sussex makes a great place to stop and enjoy afternoon tea in cosy cafés or pub lunches in entrancing countryside settings. The Three Horseshoes Pub at Elsted in Sussex is worth singling out as it has everything a great pub should have. An idyllic and historic setting, flagstones and low beamed ceilings, excellent and imaginative food washed down by cask-conditioned, local ales and specialities. Blazing fires in Winter, picnic-style tables in Summer set in a tranquil garden with a marvellous view and hens wandering freely. And of course a couple of local "characters" to prop up the bar.

Thanks to celebrated chef, Rick Stein, the Cornish resort of Padstow now attracts gastronomists from far and wide. As well as owning a local hotel and restaurants, he also runs the Padstow Seafood School and has been instrumental in getting the Brits to enjoy cooking and eating fish again. Strange to think that a country surrounded by the sea could ever have lost interest in fish.

The West Country offers plenty of their own culinary pleasures. Wiltshire ham, cheddar which actually tastes like cheese (there are now more than 400 British cheeses) rather than some of the foreign imitations, cider, Cornish pasties, clotted cream....

It's becoming easier and easier to find these regional specialities and to enjoy fresh produce as farmers bring the countryside to town and participate in farmers markets. Supposedly an incarnation of an American idea, these markets are really a throw back to earlier times (before America even existed!) when farmers brought their produce to the people who lived in towns. This latest version of farmers' markets only allow local producers to sell their own produce and there are strict restrictions as to how far producers are allowed to travel to sell their wares. The first was held in Bath in 1997 and there are now over 350 where you are likely to find seasonal vegetables, fruit, fresh meats, honey, bread, cheeses, beer, wine, relishes and pies.

FOOD FROM FAR AWAY

Some of the food we now enjoy has its origins in far off places. The end of October will see us celebrating "World Curry Week" when we'll probably be eating even more of what has supposedly become our national dish. Chicken Tikka Massala is apparently not really an Indian dish, but an Anglo-Indian creation which adapted Indian curries for more Western tastes. Whatever the case, eating ethnic food is very popular in England and we're becoming more aware of the best places to sample it. Tours are already available in Leicester, Birmingham and London to help visitors enjoy curries and to shop for spices and other ingredients not always found elsewhere.

One or two of the Bangladeshi restaurants in Brick Lane in London's East End even offer the chance to learn from the professionals with "Cook Your Own Curry Nights". It is interesting that whereas all curries were simply referred to as "Indian", English curry fans are now becoming more discriminating and choosing between the diverse cuisines of India, Bangladesh and Pakistan and starting to show an interest in the Hindu, Sikh and Muslim cultures that have shaped the food on offer.

THE ESSENCE OF "ENGLISHNESS" – PUBS

One of the aspects of life which sets England apart from other countries are its pubs. According to the British Beer and Pub Association there are about 60,000 pubs in Britain, all of them different in some way. Overseas visitors used to waiter service at their table have to get accustomed to buying their drinks directly at the bar and learning the delicate art of attracting the barmaid or barman's attention without "pushing in" or being loud. There's the added challenge of recognising the varied merits of 'bitter' (purposefully not served ice cold so the flavour comes through) and 'lager' – which is a more recent arrival from the continent.

The Roman's contribution to our road system during their occupation from around 55 BC-410 AD is well documented. Fewer people realise that this is probably when English pubs really began. The Romans developed a network of inns which offered lodging and refreshment to workers and travellers.

The King of Wessex apparently established legal ale houses in the 7th century but the main contributors to the English pub were monks. The connection between pope and pub may not seem an obvious one. Yet it was the early Christians who first offered weary travellers hospitality in their monasteries.

As time went by separate places for drinking, eating and gathering were established. Together with churches, pubs and taverns became the focal point for many communities. Even today the smallest village is almost certain to have at least one pub and church vying for popularity.

Pub signs are often a source of amusement to visitors who wonder how such strange names came into being. It was the Romans who began hanging signs outside buildings to indicate the profession of the inhabitants. For example a picture of the Roman god of Bacchus would symbolise a wine merchant. This practice continued through the ages, using simple illustrations which the largely illiterate population could recognise.

Early pub names were often religious, such as "The Cross" or "Crossed Keys" (emblem of St. Peter) or influenced by local landowners. The red lion was the personal badge of the Duke of Lancaster (one of the most powerful men in the 14th century) and later also of King James I so there were, and still are, many pubs called the "Red Lion".

Richard II decreed that all London innkeepers should use his sign of the White Hart – a pub name which is still found in many areas of London today. Names like the "Royal Oak" refer to the Oak in which King Charles II hid from his enemies.

There are plenty of pubs named after famous battles and admirals. Other pub names refer to special events or local features such as the "Railway", "Smugglers' Arms" or "Cricketers".

Of course not all pub names actually date back to the origins they seem to indicate. Sometimes new pubs are built and old names given to them, or they simply use allusions to old names. There are numerous pubs in the Firkin Brewery chain which all have the word "firkin" in them – such as "The Fowl and Firkin". A Firkin is a type of beer barrel. Some modern pubs are simply attention seeking and deliberately choose odd names as in the chain of pubs called "Slug and Lettuce".

Traditionalists dislike these modern names as they are more marketing ploys than signs with a history. There's even an Inn Sign Society for people who want to try to retain the quirky old signs and names.

PUB GAMES

Pub games are less popular than they used to be but in older country pubs you are still likely to find various traditional games being played. More modern pubs also try to attract regulars with pub quizzes, which are often fiercely debated and contested.

Darts is probably the most common game to be found and many pubs still have a darts team which competes with those from other pubs. This game probably dates back to the Middle Ages and is an indoor version of archery. It is thought that originally the target would have been the end of a barrel. Nowadays darts is played with a purpose made target board hung on a wall and with metal darts with a "flight" on the end.

Dominoes is considered to be a very English game but it actually came from Italy in the 1800s. There are 28 black and white tiles, each marked with a combination of dots and blanks from double six to double blank. These tiles are distributed to players face down. One piece is exposed and players take it in turn to match one or the other end of it. The first player to use their last piece is the winner.

Cribbage is a pub game played with two to four people with playing cards and the score is kept with pegs on a special board.

Skittles is a popular game in the counties of Gloucestershire and Somerset. There are many varieties of the game, played both indoor and outdoors and sometimes even in a miniature version on a table. The aim of the game is roughly similar in that a ball is used to knock down the skittles or "pins".

Quoits or 'horseshoes' is another ancient game which involves throwing horseshoe shaped rings at a pin usually staked in the ground. Other games which used to be popular but are now rarely seen include table games of Nine Men's Morris and Shove Ha' Penny.

Most people associate the National Trust with historic houses. It also owns over 30 working pubs, ranging widely in age and style. Some of the older inns in their care include the King's Head at Aylesbury, Buckinghamshire, a Tudor inn dating from about 1455 which retained the original courtyard and Great Hall, with stained glass featuring the coat of arms of Henry VI. The George in the medieval village of Lacock, Wiltshire is well-worth visiting for its wonderful atmosphere and typical English setting, as is The Fleece Inn at Bretforton near Evesham. This half-timbered medieval farmhouse has barely changed since it became a pub in 1848.

To find out more about beer and brewing, you can visit several museums or join a brewery tour. The National Museum of Brewing is in Burton-upon-Trent in central England.

CIDER AND PERRIES

Some areas of the country are better known for their cider (made from apples) and perry (made from pears). There is a designated National Collection of Cider at Middle Farm near Lewes in East Sussex which has the world's largest selection of ciders and perries under one roof, produced at small farms from Kent to Cornwall and Shropshire to Somerset.

The county best known for its cider is Herefordshire which produces around 60 million gallons of cider (over half the UK production) every year. The Herefordshire Cider Route follows a circular route of 60 miles. Recommended more for passengers than drivers it features six cider makers open to the public where you can sample the results as well as taking in unspoilt scenery, pretty villages and attractive old towns such as Ross-on-Wye and Leominster.

TIME FOR TEA

England is of course famous for its tea drinking and afternoon tea. By 1750 tea had become the principal drink of the middle classes in Britain. But it was still so expensive that in grand houses, the upper classes would use the tea leaves and then give them to their servants to use, who often sold the third-hand tea leaves to other villagers. Nowadays of course tea is affordable to all, with its own traditions and language.

Younger people may casually throw a tea bag into a tea cup and pour over water then milk, but those who enjoy a real 'cuppa' will tell you that you must use a teapot which has been warmed before use. Into this you should add one spoonful of tea per person and 'one for the pot'. It is important that freshly boiled water is used. After the tea has 'brewed', (or 'mashed' if you come from Yorkshire) it is poured into a cup and tea is always added to milk, never the other way round. My mother swears that tea tastes far better in a china cup and saucer than a thick mug, and drinking tea from a polystyrene cup is tantamount to a sin.

Surprisingly afternoon tea isn't quite so popular as our overseas visitors believe nor performed as well as might be expected. But when it's done well it is a real delight. Part of the enjoyment comes from its service and setting. In fact, afternoon tea is the exact antithesis of fast food. It is served by polite and discrete staff who would shy away from any form of scripted greetings although they are well aware of the 'right thing to do'.

The setting and ambience are almost as important as the actual food and tea. In Winter you can relish sitting by a cosy open fire and in Summer perhaps outdoors on a sunny terrace surrounded by lavender bushes. And above all, there is a sense of occasion and the knowledge that it is meant to take quite a while and you have plenty of chance to gossip...

Afternoon tea is traditionally served with a wide choice of different teas in silver tea pots, with proper china tea-cups and plates, starched white linen napkins and with the sandwiches and pastries beautifully displayed on a layered silver tray.

Dainty thin sandwiches are filled with cucumber, cream cheese, salmon, and egg mayonnaise. As an extra touch of gentility, the crusts are cut off. These are followed by scones with clotted cream and home-made jam, and finally a selection of cakes and pastries.

Traditional hotels are often the best places to go to enjoy afternoon tea at its best which is perhaps why overseas visitors sometimes understand its pleasures better than the English. In London, The Waldorf, Ritz and Browns Hotels offer excellent

afternoon teas. Shoppers at Fortnum and Mason enjoy a break in their tea rooms. My favourite is Cannizaro House Hotel in Wimbledon which has a cosy lounge in Winter and open terrace in Summer, looking out onto beautiful parkland.

Betty's Tea Rooms in York and Harrogate are some of the best known places to enjoy these indulgences, enjoying a world-wide reputation and drawing visitors from all over the world. Drinking a cup of tea or coffee and choosing a cake or pastry from a heavily laden trolley is not one of the world's greatest sins but the English have perfected the art of making such simple self-indulgence seem just a little 'naughty' and therefore all the more pleasurable. The genteel setting and old-fashioned looking waiters and waitresses add to the sense of escaping from the modern world for at least a short time.

Life Is Uncertain – Eat Dessert First

But before we all rush off to various areas of England to enjoy these gastronomic pleasures, anyone who enjoys cakes and sweet things should bear in mind the words of a poster I once saw: 'Life is uncertain – eat dessert first…' If this is your motto, then the Pudding Club at Three Ways House Hotel near Chipping Camden in the Cotswolds is for you.

Founded in 1985 to ensure the future of traditional delights such as Jam Roly Poly, Syrup Sponge, Sticky Toffee Pudding and Spotted Dick, the Pudding Club has an annual Great British Pudding Club Festival and regular 'meetings' of the Pudding Club' itself, usually on the 1st and 3rd Friday of each month. The evening 'meetings' begin with the rules of the club, followed by a choice of three main courses before seven traditional puddings are paraded before you. These might include well known favourites like Syrup Sponge or the more obscure Lord Randall's Pudding. Whatever the selections, you will have the opportunity to choose from the pudding buffet as often as you wish – until you say 'Enough'….

Local Specialities To Look Out For

This is by no means an exhaustive list but gives an indication of some of the local specialities you might like to look out for and sample…

Black Pudding – Particularly enjoyed in Lancashire, a sausage made from dried pig's blood

Cornish Pasties – Made from pastry and containing meat and vegetables, and sometimes fruit at one end, Cornish Pasties were taken as packed lunches by miners, farmers and fishermen. They're now enjoyed by everyone but purists fiercely debate the right recipe.

Lancashire Hot Pot – A stew, cooked slowly in the oven (as it traditionally uses cheaper cuts of meat) consisting of meat and vegetables

Melton Mowbray Pork Pies – Pork baked in hand-raised pastry – real ones only come from Melton Mowbray. Dishes of meat cooked in pastry date back to Roman times when the pastry wasn't necessarily eaten but used as a way of carrying and preserving meat on long journeys.

Pan Haggerty – A Northumbrian speciality made from pan-fried layers of potatoes, onions and meat

Parkin – Mainly available in Northern England (or at least the best is!), this spicy cake combining oatmeal and ginger is traditionally enjoyed around Guy Fawkes night (5th November)

Scouse – A liverpudlian stew made from the cheapest cuts of meat, usually mutton, boiled with potatoes and onions and often served with red cabbage pickled in vinegar. If meat is not included it is known as Blind Scouse. **Irish Stew** is a more commonly used name for the same dish.

Stargazy Pie – Herrings are cooked whole in a pie, with their heads looking skyward and tails in the middle

Yorkshire Pudding – The best ones in the Whole World are made by my mum! Consisting of a light batter of flour, eggs and milk/water perfect Yorkshire Puddings are made in a hot oven and cooked in pre-heated fat. 'Mucky Puddings' also contain onions and herbs. 'Toad-in-a-hole' is an extension of this, using the same batter recipe, with sausages laid in the batter before it is baked.

More information:

Betty's Tea Rooms
www.bettysandtaylors.co.uk
Tel: 01904 659142

Brick Lane Restaurants
(curry houses)
www.bricklanerestaurants.com

British Beer & Pub Association
www.beerandpub.com

English Wine
www.englishwineproducers.com

Guide to Cookery Courses
Published by Metro Publications
Tel: 020 8533 0922 to order

Herefordshire Cider Route
www.herefordshirecider.org.uk
Tel: 01432 260 621

National Collection of Cider
www.middlefarm.com
Tel: 01323 811 411

National Federation of Farmers' Markets
www.farmersmarkets.net

National Museum of Brewing
www.bass-museum.com
Tel: 0845 600 0598

The National Trust
www.nationaltrust.org.uk

Padstow Seafood School
www.rickstein.com
Tel: 01841 533466

Potato Tasting Festival
www.giffordshall.co.uk
Tel: 01284 830464.

The Pudding Club
www.puddingclub.com
Tel: 01386 438429

Three Horseshoes Pub
Elsted, Sussex
Tel: 01730 825746

Useful websites:

www.camra.org.uk
Campaign for Real Ale

www.eatanddrink.co.uk
Wide range of reviews, suggestions and articles

www.gofortea.com
Gives a good overview of hotels serving afternoon tea including former palaces, castles and stately homes which serve tea to non-residents

www.theaa.com
Features a restaurant & pub finder

When Napoleon declared England to be a 'nation of shop keepers' he can have had little idea of the many forms that shops were going to take. High Streets are now full of branded goods, retail chains, supermarkets, malls and other places to spend money. Anyone seeking some retail therapy has plenty of choice. People travel miles just to shop. Whereas in Napoleon's time, shopping was presumably limited to the basic necessities of life, it's now often the focal point of a trip. Coaches regularly bear hordes of visitors travelling from one town to another in search of ever better bargains.

Markets are a great draw. Maybe it's their slight mystique, a sense of mystery because no-one has a precise idea of what bargains the traders have in store. London alone has over 300 markets so they're clearly still popular. Part of the appeal is the opportunity to banter with some of the more colourful characters. Some markets are becoming more specialised and offering specific products for sale on certain days, such as fashion or antiques.

Dedicated shoppers now 'benefit' from ever larger shopping centres, often taking on the form of mini-towns with shops interspersing restaurants in major purpose-built centres such as Bluewater in Kent and Meadowhall outside Sheffield. These temples of commerce have become destinations in their own right and some even provide children's entertainers so parents can get on with the serious business of spending their money.

Shopping in these huge malls is now a leisure activity, attracting millions of visitors every year but many people dislike this type of shopping experience. The shops can seem predictable and full of similarly branded goods, with piped 'muzak' playing in an attempt to jolly customers into a happy spending mood. The air is usually so stale and warm that visitors find themselves wishing for bed almost as soon as they arrive.

Supporting Small Shops

Within more traditional towns, most shops are clustered around the 'High Street' and they generally differ from town to town. In smaller towns when a new big name store opens there's a stir of anticipation amongst residents. They feel that their town is now on the map and been brought into the 21st century. When a second chain store opens this seems to represent even more choice. The new smart stores start to make some of the older shops look a little outdated and old-fashioned.

Most residents feel happy when it looks like their town is looking better and more modern. A few people will resist the change but are dismissed as 'old-fashioned'. Rents go up so that some of the smaller shops who can't afford to pay more have to close down. Chain stores with aggressive expansion plans replace them. And so the march into the future goes on. This is progress. It's what happens.

And then you look for something special or different. But you can't find it because the shops now all sell similar things. They're paying high rents and their buying is done by some-one in a head office and there really isn't much room for indi-viduals to make their mark and offer different products. Every product sold in these more modern shops needs to sell in thousands to justify its carefully planned space on the shelf…

By this time it's pretty hard to bring back some of the more unusual shops and their quirky individual characters. So you have to go shopping in another town.

And in that town, some-one realises they are getting quite a lot of visitors so it makes sense to open a coffee shop. Just a small place, with a few seats and great atmosphere if rather erratic service. It does really well. The landlord notices, senses an opportunity, and increases the rent. But the coffee shop isn't doing so well it can afford the increase. It will have to close. Or the owners could cash in on their success and sell it – to Starbucks…

And so that town with the quirky shops and interesting things to buy starts to change. A chain store does a feasibility study and looks at the demographics and realises that now is the time to open a new shop in that town…

Moral of the story? Support the independent shops when-ever you can, appreciate their quirks and avoid the chains when-ever you can even if it isn't always so convenient. Quick, before it's too late.

Curious Customs & Impromptu Shopping

When travelling around, it's worth leaving the motorways and finding routes off the beaten track, or avoiding big towns in favour of smaller, lesser known ones. This is where you're more likely to find small local shops and ad hoc events.

The Summer and Autumn months are a great time for a more spontaneous kind of shopping, 'why don't we just stop here for a while – you never know what we might find.' And where better to find it than driving down an English country lane!

You'll stumble across farm shops and impromptu stalls with an honesty box selling anything from fresh asparagus to cherries and plants. If you travel at the right time of year, there's also a good chance you'll come across a village fete or 'fayre'.

The sense of serendipity adds to the pleasure of finding local colour. Almost every English village is proud of its ability to hold at least an annual event called the Village Fete, Fair or Fayre. These events usually combine stalls where you can buy things with games and various challenges.

Expect to find fun events like face painting, the chance to guess the weight of a cake or name of the teddy bear and old-fashioned favourites like 'Splat the Rat'. The latter is a deceptively simple game whereby a fake rat is dropped through a drainpipe fastened to a slanting board and you are challenged to take one hit at it with a hammer, to 'splat' it as it emerges. It's amazing how few people score a hit so if you want to impress the audience you might want to practise at home…

The Village Fete is almost always in aid of a good cause such as the repair of the leaking church roof, which means there are plenty of opportunities to spend money. Regulars actually queue before the gates open so they can be certain to grab their bargain or one of Auntie Maude's famous fruit cakes which she bakes every year for the occasion. You can usually buy a whole range of home-made cakes, pickles, jams and other items not found in shops. And there is sure to be a 'bric-a-brac' stall (NOT to be confused with the stuff sold at the Autumn Jumble Sale, where anything not sold today will finally end up).

The regulars queuing at the gates make a habit of dashing straight to the cake stall (this one always sells out first) and then to the bric-a-brac where there is always a good chance that they'll pay just 50 pence for a piece of pottery that will become a family heirloom. So if you have a nose for a bargain don't hesitate to join in the mêlée and pick out your own special memento from the motley collection of objects likely to be sold on the bric-a-brac stall.

Many villages and allotment societies host annual produce shows which are not dissimilar in atmosphere from the village fair. These are usually closely contested competitions which offer a swift glimpse into village life. Years of rivalry and secret tricks go into growing produce for the different classes at the show. You'll see every imaginable category – massive cabbages, the most fragrant roses and tasty carrots with their green fronds intact.

The carefully arranged produce is displayed for the judges to see. Once the cards declaring 'First', 'Second', 'Third' and 'Highly Commended' have been awarded, the public rush in to admire the results of the last few months of gardening labours and insiders' advice. You can always spot the people who have entered the competition. They turn up every year without fail and have practised the art of casually dashing to see their plates of produce without actually seeming to be in a hurry to know the results.

Part of the appeal of these events is that they are local and uncommercial so they're not always publicised outside the area. You're most likely to find details of them on church notice boards or look at the postcards in newsagents windows which always give a fascinating insight into the type of neighbourhood you're in. Local Tourist Information Centres are usually a good place to find out more.

If you enjoy this sort of small-scale, local event you'll probably also enjoy WI (short for Women's Institute) Markets. They started in 1919 to provide a place where surplus homemade and home-grown produce could be sold to the general public and are now held in about 500 locations through-out Great Britain. They are usually held for one morning a week and all money made goes back to the producer.

The products you're most likely to see at these weekly events are craft work (helping to keep traditional skills alive) and homemade food, as well as homegrown vegetables, plants and flowers. The atmosphere is very friendly and you're bound to receive well-meant advice from the seller about the goods you buy as the sellers take great pride in their creations and produce. It's always worth arriving early as they nearly always sell out before the allocated closing time.

SHOPPING BY THE SEA

For a totally different shopping experience, head for the coastal towns, especially some of the more traditional ones. Make sure you are hungry when you arrive so you can enjoy fish and chips in the open air (even in the rain, they taste much better this way) at the coast.

The sights and smells are usually in sharp contrast to inland towns and for me evoke nostalgic memories of childhood holidays. Brightly coloured postcards, buckets, and deckchairs battle for space with seashells, souvenirs, and sticky rock. There's always plenty of "tat" for sale, offering plenty of chances to speculate what kind of person would really want to pay good money to take it home with them.

FAIRS AND EXHIBITIONS

The appeal of finding something that isn't available elsewhere is strong. Craft fairs attract huge crowds of people, all searching for the chance to buy hand-made products directly from the person who made them. Until recently most of them were fairly small events with a handful of craftspeople from around the area. Now inspired by the wealth of magazines and television programmes dedicated to home improvements, they are growing and attracting more and more visitors.

The annual Living Crafts event at Hatfield House in Hertfordshire in May is one of the largest gatherings of craftspeople in Europe. It includes an awe-inspiring range of demonstrations and chances to participate. Crafts include glass-blowing, woodcarving, blacksmiths, quilting, silk-painting, lace-making, bodging, hedge-laying, charcoal burning and other woodland crafts.

Anyone looking to spot the latest trends, newest gadgets, fashions and products of the future will love the combination of exhibition and shopping offered by a growing range of events taking place in high profile venues like the NEC in Birmingham or various London exhibition halls. Events such as The Ideal Homes Exhibition, Good Food Show, and Gardeners World Live capitalise on our growing interest in home improvements, gardening and cooking.

Exhibition venues of the more traditional variety such as museums and galleries are often a great place to find unusual products and items not sold in the shops. Museums and galleries are increasingly seeing their shops as major money-makers and sourcing products from all over the world to tie in with special events or exhibitions and generate essential income. The Science Museum (see page 150) has a fantastic shop with great things for children some of which are educational and others that are just good fun. Most of the time you don't even need to pay to see the exhibition or visit the museum if you want to just shop. They are mainly open to the public during usual trading hours and are ideal when you're looking to buy gifts with a difference.

ANTIQUES AND OTHER FINDS

Collectors of curios and antiques will rarely find a better place to shop than in England. You can choose from a host of auction houses, salvage yards and specialist dealers. London's Portobello Road is apparently the world's largest antiques market. Some 1500 traders set up their stalls and shops every Saturday and the "Lane" as it is locally known certainly attracts more than its fair share of antique hunters.

You are more likely to find bargains elsewhere – either in the North of England where prices are much lower or by trying to shop where the dealers are known to go. Set your alarm clock, take a torch and try the delights of Bermondsey Square market just South of Tower Bridge early on a Friday morning. It starts at 4.00 am and finishes around 11.00 am but dealers know that the best bargains are to be found before daybreak… It's said that dealers buy their stock here and sell it at double the price on the Portobello Road the next day.

Another fascinating place to explore which feels like you're stumbled upon an insiders' secret is the London Silver Vaults in Chancery Lane in London. A myriad of specialist silverware dealers sell an incredible range of goods from tiny pieces of jewellery to big brash candelabras. All the dealers are downstairs in the vaults behind huge safe doors and seem willing to advise both browsers and buyers.

If you want to be sure you're dealing with a reputable antique dealer, look out for one of the 400 members of the British Antique Dealers' Association.

For antiques on a physically large scale, try a visit to an architectural salvage yard. These Aladdin's Caves are the places to find doors, garden statues, gargoyles, fireplaces and even whole staircases. If you have the space, a visit to Lassco's Warehouse in East London is a must. It even sells fittings and furniture from pubs, municipal buildings and churches as well as circus and fairground paraphernalia.

More information:

Architectural Salvage
www.salvo.co.uk

Bermondsey Square and its street market
www.bermondsey-square.com

British Antique Dealers' Association
www.bada.org.
Tel: 020 7589 4128

Chancery Lane Silver Vaults
www.thesilvervaults.com
Tel: 020 7242 3844

Craft Fair at Hatfield House
www.livingcrafts.co.uk
Tel: 023 9242 6523

The London Architectural Salvage & Supply Company
www.lassco.co.uk

Portobello Antique Dealers' Association
www.portobelloroad.co.uk

WI markets
www.wimarkets.co.uk

ONLY IN ENGLAND – LOCAL DISTINCTIVENESS

For such a small country, England offers huge diversity. Some fairly major regional differences can be found within a short journey, giving each area a distinct character. Expressed through varied landscapes, accents, dialects, customs, food, and even lifestyles and religion, this is part of what makes touring England so worthwhile.

Some of the contrasts are obvious – compare the view from England's highest mountain, Scafell Pike in the Lake District, with the apparent closeness of the huge sky over the flat Fenlands in East Anglia.

Other differences are tiny and only noticed by those in the know. These smaller variations are nonetheless important to local people as they define the place where they live. My secondary school had a catchment area of around 3 miles. To outsiders there were no discernable differences between the pupils from each village, and yet we were instinctively aware through almost indescribable nuances of dialect and accent, whether fellow pupils were from our village or 'across the valley'. At Christmas time visitors to my village don't recognise some of the carols sung in the Church – they are only sung in that one village.

It's often only by travelling around the country or moving to a new area, that one appreciates the extent of England's diversity and its local distinctiveness. Touring around, one becomes aware of the differences in landscape, from the soft rolling hills of the Sussex Downs to the wild Cornish coves, craggy outcrops of the Peak District, open Salisbury Plain or brooding Cheviot Hills in Northumbria.

Some of the regional differences are created by man and have evolved through more than 2000 years of history. We use age-old building materials and methods dating back centuries, taking advantage of whatever is locally available.

Simply looking at the buildings around you can reveal what part of the country you're in. Bath has its distinctive yellow limestone, many Northern towns their red brick or stern granite, and East Anglia its pastel coloured pargetting. Even roofs give clues to our location whether they are grey slate, curvy pantiles or picturesque thatches. Excellent open air attractions like the Weald and Downland Museum in West Sussex provide a record of the many different building styles and materials which have been used in England through-out the ages and aid an appreciation of the finer points of our architecture. They have painstakingly moved and re-erected buildings at risk from all over the country.

DECIPHERING PLACE NAMES

England has been invaded by various groups of people and they have all left their mark in some way. The Celts, Romans, Anglo-Saxons, Scandinavians and French have all influenced our place names. They often give clues about the past and how a place came to be or what made someone settle there, although it's impossible to be totally accurate. By breaking place names down into several syllables you will often be able to spot some of the following.

Most Celtic place names are found in the North and West, particularly in Cornwall. Meanings include:

> Aber – mouth of a river
> Coombe – deep valley
> Glen – narrow valley
> Pen – a hill

Romans often seemed to use existing Celtic place names but they did add some Latin elements of their own such as:

> Chester or caster (from Castra) – roman fort or town
> Coln (from Colonia) – a settlement
> Port (from porta or portus) – a gate or harbour
> Street or strat (from strata) – road

The Anglo-Saxons gave us old English words such as:

> Borne – brook or stream
> Dun – hill
> Ey – island
> Ham – homestead
> Hamm – water meadow or enclosure

Ing (from ingas) – the people of
Ley – a clearing
Stede – place or site of building
Ton – town or village
Well – well
Worth – enclosure or homestead

Names like –ham and –hamm show why it is impossible to always be accurate in determining origins. Over the years names become altered and abbreviated so places that now end in –ham may well have started life as a –hamm, although it's also probable that many homesteads were built in the same places as enclosures and water meadows.

The Vikings left Scandinavian place names such as

By – a farm, or village
Dalr – valley or dale
Gil – ravine
Holm – flat ground by river
Thorpe – farm or small settlement
Thwaite – meadow
Toft – plot of land or site for building

By the time the Normans invaded in 1066 many settlements and place names were established so although French was the language of the English parliament for three centuries, it had less of an effect on English place names. Their influence is still seen though in names of abbeys such as Jervaulx and Rievaulx in Yorkshire.

LOOKING FOR CLUES TO THE PAST

There's an enormous satisfaction to be derived from looking
more closely at our surroundings and following clues that
reveal local history and a way of life, that others might easily
overlook.

Even small features can unveil details about the location.
Examine the knockers on fine Georgian buildings and you'll
see a clue to the house's past. In Spitalfields in East London,
many door-knockers are in the form of a hand with lace
around the wrist, telling of the Huguenot silk-weavers who
brought their craft to the area. In coastal towns of a similar
era like Rye, you're more likely to find symbols relating to fish
and the sea. Such details are often missed by people who
scurry by.

Many of the signs of local distinctiveness are starting to disap-
pear as tasks become automated and more products are mass
produced but they are still evident in some parts of the countryside. Old gates to fields in Gloucester and Devon look
quite different from each other, using varied systems of cross
bars and verticals. Before the advent of combine harvesters,
every area used to have its own way of making a haystack,
sometimes square, sometimes round.

Different areas of the country have their own ways of dividing
up fields. In many areas of the Lake District and Peak District,
fields are divided by dry-stone walls for no better reason than
there were so many stones in the field. But these walls look
very different from the Herringbone patterned ones of
Cornwall and the landscape is given a quite changed look
when fields are divided by hedgerows as they are more likely
to be in Kent, often mixing many different varieties of trees,
plants and shrubs.

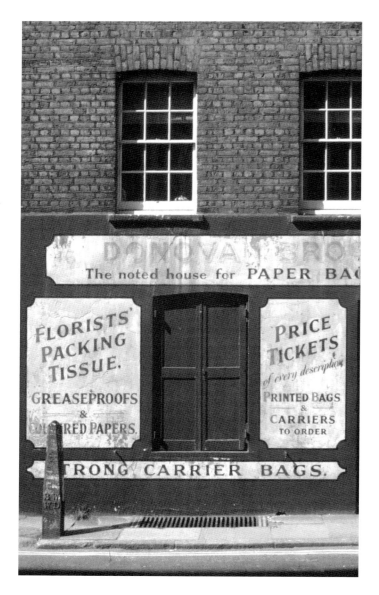

ATTRACTIONS AND CUSTOMS

England isn't short of attractions demonstrating regional differences and the history and circumstances which make one area different from another, whether in the town or countryside.

You can watch hops being harvested at the Museum of Kent Life or find out more about local witches at Ryedale Folk Museum. Many museums celebrate the industry that contributed to the growth of particular areas, whether this was tin mining in Cornwall or growing Lavender in Norfolk. The Ironbridge Gorge Museum in the Midlands shows how life was changed through the industrial revolution.

Thanks to increased enjoyment of food and interest in how it is produced, local foods are enjoying a renaissance. As you travel around England, trying the local delicacy is an added pleasure, especially if its slightly indulgent like a clotted cream tea in Devon or fresh oysters in Whitstable. Some of the country's attractions help to preserve our food heritage such as the Brogdale Trust, home to the National Fruit Collections, which includes over 2300 different varieties of apples! Individuals also play their part. The 'Pumpkin Man' in Slindon, West Sussex is a draw to locals and visitors from miles around but you will have to visit to understand – ask a local and they'll point you in the right direction!!

Local customs also contribute to our sense of place and can be a great incentive for a visit. You can still witness the Pearly Kings and Queens of London at their Harvest Festival service on the 1st Sunday in October at St. Martin's in the Field (see page 136) or enjoy watching the Furry Dance in Helston, Cornwall (see page 130). The Peak District Well Dressings take place at various locations through-out the Summer. Other customs take place at a set time of year such as Apple

Day in October, in various areas but particularly worth visiting in Much Marcle, Herefordshire.

If you are travelling around England and want to appreciate local customs and England's regional diversity, a good place to start is the Tourist Information Centre for that particular area, where staff are likely to be armed with excellent local knowledge.

A brief look at just some of the events taking place on or around May Day (1st May) gives an insight into the enormous variety of ways of celebrating a single day across England. May Day is a centuries-old tradition which was originally a pagan fertility rite dating back as early as 238 BC. It was a Roman festival in celebration of Floralia – the goddess of flowering and blossoming.

In Oxford the festivities start at dawn with singing by the Magdalen College choir. Students and other onlookers gather in their thousands on and around the Magdalen Bridge, remaining until morning when the crowd disperses into the surrounding streets and celebrations continue with music and Morris dancing.

Maypole and Morris dancing are among the activities associated with this time of year. Morris dancers can be seen in many country villages during the summer months performing dances that once held ritualistic and magical meanings associated with the awakening of the earth. The costume varies from team to team, but basically consists of white trousers, a white shirt, bells worn around the calf of the leg, and a hat made of felt or straw, decorated with ribbons and flowers. The bells and ribbons are said to banish harm and bring fertility. In some dances the dancers will use sticks which they clash in time to the music.

Morris dancers are the main source of entertainment at Cerne Abbas when they and their followers gather on the Cerne Giant. The entertainment is somewhat stranger in Padstow. The town is decorated with the first greenery of the year, bluebells and hazel twigs and there is a 'obby Oss' (hobby horse) in a procession with dancers, singers and musicians to celebrate the coming of spring. The dance's origins are believed to be pagan and it is one of the oldest remaining customs in England. Similar events take place in Minehead in Somerset.

In Tetbury at the edge of the Cotswolds, there is another strange event when locals arrange themselves into teams of four and in pairs, they relay a 60lb woolsack up and down a hill. There's a procession of a different kind in Castleton in the Peak District – the Ancient Garland Ceremony in which the Garland King carries a bell-shaped garland of flowers to the market by horse-back. Each of these activities dates back centuries and is continued as part of the festivities which mark one village or town out from another.

ENGLAND IN PARTICULAR

The charity, Common Ground is gathering material for a new book which will be launched in May 2005 called, "England in Particular". The idea is to gather local stories, legends, customs, recipes and other information which is important to people living in England and which marks one community or area out from another.

Common Ground ask, "What tells you where you are? What are the visual clues in the buildings, streets, fields, hedgerows, stonewalls, trees, lanes, streams, pubs? What do the names of the places, fields and streams mean? What of the seasons, floods, first swallows, festivals, recipes, songs? What of the animals — domestic breeds of dog, sheep, cow, pig? What about fruit and veg, grain and crops of all kinds, do any hail from your place?

There are so many cultures represented across England in country and city, some with us for centuries, some very new. What impact have they had in the design of buildings, the words we use, our produce, what we eat, the customs and colours of life?"

By collating the commonplace things that are often taken from granted and yet which are absolutely vital to mark local differences, it is hoped the book will celebrate them and help to preserve them for the future. For Common Ground contact details see page 94. Their website is an excellent source of information about particular localities, events and English customs.

CRICKET

It would be impossible to talk about all things English without mentioning the game of cricket for which England is famous, although other nationalities now play it much better than us!

Cricket is a quintessentially English game, dating back to the 14th century. To the outsider it is an often slow and boring pastime, bound up with tradition and strange terminology. Part of the joy of cricket matches is linked to their often very pleasant setting on a village green and preferably close to a pub, joined by friends. A rough understanding of the rules will also make it more enjoyable – the following might help.

There are two teams of eleven players who play in 'cricket whites' – clothes which are actually more cream than white. Each of the teams also includes two umpires or referees.

Cricket is played in a field which is oval – hence the name the 'Oval' for the cricket ground in Vauxhall. The middle of the field is where the main 'action' takes place. This 'pitch' should be hard and dry (hence the consternation when it rains). At each end of the pitch is a 'wicket', consisting of three vertical poles called 'stumps' and two small horizontal sticks (bails) resting on top of them. The cricket bat is oblong shaped with a thinner handle and made out of willow. The ball is quite heavy and made of cork, covered in leather and then stitched. It really hurts if you get hit by it!

To begin one team bats and the other team 'fields' or 'bowls'. The fielding team are spread out over the field getting ready to catch the ball, except for the bowler. Two batsman from the same team stand at different ends of the pitch, one facing the bowler from the other team. The bowler runs up to the pitch where he bowls the ball over arm. He releases the ball before he reaches the white line painted on the pitch called the 'crease'. If he steps over this he gets a one run penalty. The aim of the bowler is to hit the wicket whereas the batsman tries to protect the wicket and to score 'runs' by hitting the ball.

'Runs' are the way teams score. This means that when a batsman hits the ball he runs to the other end of the cricket pitch past the crease. The other batsman has to run to the opposite end as well. The batsman can run as many times as they like, but the batsmen can get out if their stumps are hit with the ball by a fielder before the batsman reaches the crease. Runs can also be scored by hitting the ball out of the field to the boundary. If the ball bounces before it reaches the edge, the batsman scores 4 runs and if it doesn't bounce he scores 6 runs.

The fielding team try to get the batsman out. He is then replaced by another member of his team until they have all been out in the field. There are four main ways of getting the batsman out. 1) if the bowler hits the wicket and knocks it down; 2) if a fielder catches the ball the batsman has hit before it reaches the ground; 3) if the ball hits any part of the batsman's body and the umpire thinks that the ball would hit the wicket if it had not hit the batsman. This is known as 'leg before wicket' or LBW; 4) if the batsman is run out – this happens if a fielder catches the ball and hits the wicket with it while the batsmen are running to the other end of the pitch.

When 10 of the players from the batting team are out, the teams swop over and the fielding team tries to beat the number of runs scored. Each team has one 'inning' of 50 'overs'. An over is a series of 6 bowls by a bowler. Each bowler can only bowl a maximum of 10 overs. If 10 of a team's batsman are out, the innings ends there regardless of how many balls are left to be bowled.

If all this sounds too complicated then perhaps it's easiest to simply remember, 'The rules of cricket as explained to a foreign visitor', an anonymous explanation often seen on souvenir tea towels. It actually gives an accurate explanation:

1) You have two sides, one out in the field and one in.

2) Each man that's in the side that's in, goes out, and when he's out, he comes in and the next man goes in until he's out.

3) When they are all out the side that's out comes in and the side that's been in goes out and tries to get those coming in out.

4) Sometimes you get men still in and not out.

5) When both sides have been in and out including the not-outs, that's the end of the game.

APPRECIATING & MAINTAINING LOCAL DISTINCTIVENESS

Here are just a few ways to start noticing local distinctiveness and perhaps enhance your enjoyment of England:

❖ As you walk along the High Street look up. Looking above the shop fronts you can ignore the monotonous brands and homogenised shops and appreciate the architecture which is often ignored. Look out for clues to former uses for the building, such as old signs and inscriptions.

❖ Look again at familiar landscapes. If you look closely you may be able to see how fields have been shaped by their previous uses. You can sometimes even recognise the ridges from medieval times when fields were divided into narrow strips.

❖ Shop in small independent shops and at farmers' markets whenever possible. Shopping can be more fun and personal this way as you get to know the people who sell to you – at farmers' markets you can find out more about where the produce comes from and the best ways of cooking it. Shopping in smaller outlets helps to keep the all-powerful monster brands at bay and makes your own shopping experience more enjoyable.

❖ Try to buy food from the places it comes from. Where better to appreciate Gloucester Old Spot (pork) than in Gloucester or Theakstons Old Peculiar (beer) than in Yorkshire?

❖ The smallest details on buildings often tell a story of their own. The size, form and details on doorways may explain their past. Look out for boot-scrapers at the side of a door or door-knockers which give clues to former owners' lives.

❖ Listen! You'll hear different local dialects and bird-song which are quite specific to that place. Listen to local stories – find out about ghosts and legends to unearth the tales of the past and how they shape the present. Local traditions are often based on ancient stories, part of which have long since been forgotten but the customs carry on.

❖ Celebrate the changes that come through-out the year – eat food as it comes into season and participate in festivals and local celebrations.

❖ When you want to remember a place or buy a souvenir try to find things that are locally made, avoiding the gifts that can be found in any standard "tourist trap" shop and which are in any case often made overseas!

❖ Consider place names – they often help you to under-stand why a place is where it is and how it developed. This in turn can help you to appreciate some of its present features and how to safeguard them.

❖ Look at how buildings are made. They often relate to the local geology and show craftsmanship which varies from place to place. A dry stone wall in the Cotswolds uses flat stones whereas in Dartmoor the stones are more rounded and uneven. Chimneys, roof shapes, gable ends, bricks, stones and even gate styles vary.

Museums, Attractions & More Information:

Brogdale Trust
www.brogdale.org.uk
Tel: 01795 535286

Common Ground
(charity promoting local distinctiveness)
www.commonground.org.uk

Events calendar
www.whatsonwhen.com

Helston Furry (Floral) Dance
www.helston-online.co.uk

Ironbridge Gorge Museum
www.ironbridge.org.uk
Tel: 01952 432 166

MCC Museum (Lord's Cricket Ground)
www.lords.org
Tel: 020 7432 1033

Museum of Kent Life
www.museum-kentlife.co.uk
Tel: 01622 763936

Pearly Kings and Queens
www.pearlies.co.uk

Ryedale Folk Museum
www.ryedalefolkmuseum.co.uk
Tel: 01751 417367

Weald and Downland Museum
www.wealddown.co.uk
Tel: 01243 811363

ENGLAND –
WHATEVER THE WEATHER

England has wonderful weather. Really, it has. Compare it to places so hot they're practically forced to close down so everyone can sleep during the mid-day heat. Or countries so cold that before you can go anywhere, you have to spend tedious minutes piling on the layers.

England's climate is mild, and the changing seasons provide colour, variety and a host of traditions associated with each one. Of course, the rain can make things a bit wet but on the whole it's a good thing. We hardly ever win the cricket or tennis but we do have the greenest, prettiest fields and tennis courts. And where would the Lake District be without rain to fill the lakes?

GARDENS GALORE

Few countries offer so many opportunities to enjoy the changing seasons and appreciate beautiful countryside and coastline. Our temperate climate has made English gardens the envy of horticulturists the world over. Almost every area has its garden-related attractions to visit, ranging from new venues such as the Eden Project and Millennium Seed Bank Project at Wakehurst (where over 24,000 species of plants are being collected and safeguarded against extinction) to long-established and much-loved places like the Royal Botanical Gardens at Kew.

It isn't only rich landowners or country house-owners who enjoy showing off their planting triumphs. How often have you strolled past a garden and wished you could take a quick peek inside, perhaps chat with the owners? This is made possible thanks to a charity called the National Gardens Scheme which arranges for more than 2000 private gardens all over England and Wales to open to the public every year. They are all in the famous 'Yellow Book' called 'Gardens of England and Wales Open for Charity', updated each year.

The temptation of sneaking a look at a garden that is normally private, combined with afternoon tea and the chance to buy some plants clearly appeals to many. The scheme is rapidly growing in popularity as more gardens are added each year. The gardens which open are of every conceivable size, shape and variety and sometimes a whole village of gardeners open their gates on the same day, adding to the friendly atmosphere. The money raised from this imaginative scheme goes to numerous charities – around £1 million is raised each year.

A clump of gardening programmes and magazines have made us into an even more green-fingered nation and there are plenty of places to go for inspiration and information. Events like the gardening shows at Hampton Court Palace, Chelsea and Tatton Park are a further impetus for Englands' gardening enthusiasts.

ACTIVE PURSUITS

Gardening is said to be one of Britain's most popular hobbies but not everyone wants to engage in such gentle pursuits. There's a massive and growing choice of outdoor pursuits available. Hardy souls and dare-devils can try white-water rafting, canoeing, abseiling and even water-skiing thanks to specialist operators around the country.

Members of the British Activity Holiday Association provide quality assured opportunities for adults and children. A range of operators offer the chance to try your hand at an almost unimaginable range of outdoor pursuits, which are often also aimed at enhancing our enjoyment of the coast and countryside. For a completely different view, and perhaps as a special treat, there are numerous ways to take to the skies from the exhilaration of flying in a Tiger Moth to the serenity of gliding or going up in a hot-air balloon. One of the easiest and safest

(insurance included) ways of buying some of these more exhil-
arating experiences is via a company such as Red Letter Days.

More sedate pursuits can be enjoyed on terra firma, and add to
our appreciation of the countryside and skills of those who
work the land. Whether you fancy hurdle-making, fashioning
garden furniture out of willow withies or learning to milk
cows, you can be assured that someone somewhere in England
wants to teach you to do so. Companies like Acorn Activities
offer a bewildering selection of activities which are proving
popular with people who wish to organise a hen or stag
weekend with a difference.

Craft fairs and special events around the country also offer an
opportunity to watch demonstrations and learn more about
potential new hobbies. Tourist Information Centres usually
have lists of events and venues.

NATIONAL PARKS

We are lucky that England not only has such a beautiful coast and countryside, but that it is well protected and signposted to help us enjoy it.

The National Parks each have their own distinctive identity and work hard to preserve the area in their care, whilst still offering the public plenty of chances to enjoy it. There are eight Parks in England: The Peak District; Lake District; Dartmoor; North York Moors; Yorkshire Dales; Exmoor; Northumberland and the Norfolk and Suffolk Broads. The first one in the Peak District was established after conflict between walkers and landowners.

In 1932 a "mass trespass" took place on Kinder Scout, with walkers defying landowners and gamekeepers because opportunities to walk on the moors were so limited. Five men were imprisoned and the fight for public access intensified. It took several years to happen but eventually the first parks were established. 1999 was the 50th anniversary of the National Parks.

CARING FOR THE COUNTRYSIDE OF THE FUTURE

Efforts are still being made to not only preserve the countryside for future generations to enjoy but also enhance it now. New community forests are being planted so that a larger proportion of the population lives within easy reach of a forest.

The National Forest is a relatively new environmental project, encouraging alternative land use by farmers and landowners.

The boundary of the Forest has been fixed so it covers 200 square miles of the English Midlands, spanning parts of Derbyshire, Leicestershire and Staffordshire. At the outset of the project, woodland covered only 6% of the area. The ultimate aim is that woodland will cover approximately a third of the area, a third will remain in agriculture with the remainder comprising towns and villages.

At the heart of the National Forest is a new award-winning visitor centre called "Conkers" which has different outdoor activities including lakeside walks, ponds, mazes, sculpture and nature trails, an assault course and wildlife watching.

SHANKS' PONY

The Ramblers Association aims to help everyone enjoy walking outdoors, whether for relatively short Sunday afternoon strolls or longer route marches across the Pennine Way. Their website and range of publications gathers together a vast selection of information on different routes, trails and themed walks over hill and dale, through towns and along the coast which people of almost any ability can enjoy, including some urban walks.

The British Tourist Authority's "Walking Britain" map is available free from its overseas offices or on the website and includes details of National Trails and other routes.

AN ISLAND OF ISLANDS

We are fortunate that being part of an island, we have a very varied coastline to enjoy. The English seaside really can be enjoyed in all weathers. Mediterranean beaches may sometimes be sunnier than ours, but few offer the added distraction of rock pools in which to watch all manner of maritime creatures.

Another attraction of the English seaside are its pleasure piers. These splendours of Victorian architecture offer shelter from the occasional shower, refreshments and old-fashioned entertainment in the form of bingo, one-armed bandits (slot machines) and Aunt Sallies. These are a real English experience and often very pleasant places to walk, despite the somewhat bracing climate.

An oft forgotten aspect of our coastline are the many islands around the perimeter of England. The Isle of Wight is said to be England in miniature and was certainly a favourite retreat from the stresses and strains of regal life for Queen Victoria. The Isle of Man is famous for the TT Motorbike Races but is also a green haven.

Some of the smaller islands can be the most entrancing. Basking in the warmth of the Gulf Stream, the Scilly Isles entice visitors with their exotic plants while Lundy attracts people to its range of Landmark Trust properties, many hoping to see its famous puffins. Puffins are among many other seabirds and seals which can be seen on the Maritime Nature Reserve of the Farne Islands, off the Northumbria coast.

More information:

Acorn Activities
www.acornactivities.co.uk
Tel: 08707 40 50 55

British Activity Holiday Association
www.baha.org.uk
Tel: 01932 252994

British Piers Society
www.piers.co.uk
Tel: 01268 757291

British Tourist Authority
(website includes special section on gardens to visit)
www.visitbritain.com

Community Forests
www.communityforest.org.uk
Tel: 01684 311880

Conkers – The National Forest Visitor Centre
www.visitconkers.com
Tel: 01283 216633

Eden Project
www.edenproject.com
Tel: 01726 811911

Isle of Wight
www.isle-of-wight-tourism.gov.uk
Tel: 01983 813818

Millennium Seed Bank Project at Wakehurst
www.rbgkew.org.uk/seedbank
Tel: 01444 894178

National Forest
www.nationalforest.org
Tel: 01283 551211

National Gardens Scheme – "Yellow Book"
www.ngs.org.uk.

National Parks
www.cnp.org.uk
Tel: 020 7924 4077

The Ramblers Association
www.ramblers.org.uk
Tel: 020 7339 8500

Red Letter Days
www.redletterdays.co.uk
Tel: 0870 444 4004

Royal Botanical Gardens at Kew
www.rbgkew.org.uk
Tel: 020 8332 5000

Royal Horticultural Society
(gardening shows at: Hampton Court Palace, Chelsea and Tatton Park)
www.rhs.org.uk
Tel: 020 7834 4333

BUTCHER, BAKER, CANDLE-STICK MAKER

What is it about watching other people work? We have a day off, time to relax and enjoy our leisure time and what do we love to do? Watch others at work. It's partly fascination and also a rather smug feeling of being lazy when others aren't. And we like to know "how do they do that?"

FRUITS OF THEIR LABOURS

I can't go past one of those wonderful seaside shops that promise "see rock being made". There are chances to see lettered rock or candy sticks being made in almost every English seaside town. You can watch rock being stretched and manipulated and then see them getting the little letters inside the candy strips to spell "Blackpool" or whatever the name of the place, before it is batched up and neatly stacked on the shelves. Probably the largest shop is at the Rock Factory Shop in Great Yarmouth which produces around 80,000 sticks of rock every week as well as huge mountains of chocolate.

Watching food or drink being produced seems to be a real favourite. Perhaps we secretly hope that a chocolate-making machine will develop a leak just as we're next to it or start shooting out free chocolate éclairs.

You can now see almost any food or drink being produced in some area of the country, ranging from several vineyards in Kent to Wensleydale Cheese at the Hawes Dairy in Yorkshire, made famous by cartoon characters, Wallace and Grommit. There was a public outcry when the dairy was in danger of being closed down and the visitor centre is now a major draw to visitors.

You can see what it means to be 'as busy as a bee' and visit a real 'hive of industry' in the form of Quince Honey Farm in South Molton in Devon which is Britain's largest working honey farm and where bees have apparently colonised a post-box, chimney and straw skeps as well as more conventional hives.

Breweries such as at Fullers and Youngs in London and Theakstons in Masham, Yorkshire are opening their doors and inviting visitors to see some of their secrets. Some breweries offer the opportunity for visitors to take a turn at brewing and return later to collect their own label beer.

Visits to factories are just as popular. These range from those with purpose-built visitor centres such as Cadbury World (which just shows the packaging plant) to those where you can watch demonstrations. At the potteries in the Midlands you're likely to see pots being thrown, fired, and painted. There's a different kind of fascination with watching designer-makers at craft fairs in the country as they demonstrate such varied skills as hurdle making and bodging, wood turning and candle-making.

LIVING ART

Artists normally shun the limelight and prefer to work away quietly in their studios but once a year in December many of them participate in the Hidden Art Open Studios event in East London. This is when many of them open to the public so you have an opportunity to see them at work and buy directly from the artists, often at a disounted price.

BELOW STAIRS

We've been enjoying tours around stately homes for many years now but for some reason, according to market research at least, we find the most interesting parts of such historic houses are the areas usually hidden to visitors. Not the grand areas where noble families may still reside, but the "working areas" like the kitchens (see Hampton Court kitchen page 164). Such is the level of interest, the National Trust has recently started to open the kitchens and "below stairs" areas of many of the buildings in their care. Perhaps we all have a sneaking suspicion that had we lived 100 years ago, we'd be more likely to have been servants than lords.

Although renowned for its care of stately homes and gardens, the National Trust has recently restored and opened a very different property. The Workhouse at Southwell in Nottinghamshire was built in 1824 and housed 158 paupers, serving as a prototype for the Poor Law of 1834. Visitors can now see the wings and yards which segregated men from women and adults from children, as well as dividing the "able bodied" from the "old and infirm". An audio guide takes visitors through the dormitories, staff quarters, wash house and other areas and a video shows how life would have been for the people living and working there.

BRINGING HISTORY TO LIFE

Another group of people facing perilous situations through their work are soldiers. English Heritage stage an amazing annual display of 2000 years of combat action. The recreation at Kirby Hall in Northamptonshire is the world's largest historical action event and takes place in mid August. More than 3000 performers recreate military action from Roman times to D-Day including infantry attacks, cavalry charges, jousting tournaments, tank battles and World War II fighter plane displays. History in Action also has areas devoted to food, clothing, entertainment, arts and crafts and other aspects of everyday life through the ages.

Historical re-enactments are popular at many industrial heritage sites and open air museums. In the North of England, Beamish offers a working experience of life as it was in the Great North in the early 1800s and 1900s set over 300 acres of beautiful countryside. Ironbridge Gorge Museum helps visitors to trace the history of an industrial revolution which changed the world.

Another 'model' (in the sense of an example, not miniature version) village can be seen at Saltaire near Bradford in Yorkshire, as England's finest example of an integrated textile mill and village.

Some of the worksites you can visit have a historical focus but are still where people actually work today. English Heritage has listed (so it is preserved for future generations to enjoy) the Jewellery Quarter of Birmingham as it is the world's most important surviving example of a 19th/20th century metal-working community. But this isn't just a historical site – around 6000 people still work in the area, usually making jewellery in small family firms and often using the original machinery.

Many of England's traditional industries are now in decline but attempts are being made to show what it was like to work in some of the huge factories and be exposed to harsh working conditions. Housed in a former steelworks between Sheffield and Rotherham in Yorkshire, Magna is a science centre which

gives an insight into such conditions. Visitors are initially dazed by the sheer scale of the machines, suspended walkways and theatrical lighting which is reminiscent of the glow of the furnaces. There is a show, called "The Big Melt" re-creating the world's largest electric arc furnace using machinery, sound, lighting and jets of flame.

Open Government

After such dramatic insights into very harsh and difficult working conditions, the more cynical among us may not regard the Houses of Parliament as a true work place, but visitors do seem to be interested in seeing the corridors of power for themselves.

In this case 'open government' now means guided tours of the chambers of both the House of Commons and the House of Lords. Tours start at the Sovereign's Entrance and include the Queen's Robing Room, the Royal Gallery, the debating chambers, and Westminster Hall which partly dates from the 11th century. The tours are conducted by specially trained blue badge guides but only take place during the Summer recess.

Behind The Scenes

The intrigue and appeal of going behind the scenes is strong. Historic houses are increasingly recognising the potential of this and offering guided tours even when houses are normally closed to the public. Chatsworth House in Derbyshire manages to make even cleaning and maintenance sound interesting by offering the chance to visit some of the working parts of the stately home with the housekeeper or other staff, taking in areas such as the cellars, roof and joiner's shop. In years to come, perhaps visitors will even be willing to pay to help dust...

Theatres recognise that visitors love the opportunity to combine the magic of the theatre and chance to see areas not normally seen by the public and now more and more of them are taking small groups of people backstage for special tours. The star of this particular show is surely Shakespeare's Globe at Bankside in London. With 'Storytellers' as your guide, the tour itself also becomes a performance, using the reconstructed theatre (it was built using similar materials and methods to the original one on that site in Shakespeare's time) as the basis for all sorts of otherwise obscure facts and nuggets of interest from Elizabethan/Jacobean times. The best time to visit is probably in the run-up to the opening of the summer season when you can see the Globe Theatre Company in full technical rehearsal.

Anyone with an interest in show business will also enjoy back-stage tours at the BBC Centre in London which usually include the Newsroom, Weather Centre and chance to see programme-making in action.

But the crown surely has to go to those energetic people who take time off from their regular employers, in order to work elsewhere on a voluntary basis. Every year a staggering 130,000 volunteers work an amazing 264,000 days with the British Trust for Conservation Volunteers on a variety of coun-tryside projects! The appeal seems to be the opportunity to make a difference, help maintain the countryside and meet like-minded individuals but it still sounds like work to me…

More Information:

BBC Centre Tours
www.bbc.co.uk/tours
Tel: 0870 603 0304

Beamish North of England Open Air Museum
www.beamish.org.uk
Tel: 0191 370 4000

Chatsworth House & Estate
www.chatsworth-house.co.uk
Tel: 01246 565300

English Heritage
www.english-heritage.org.uk
Tel: 0870 333 1181

Hidden Art Open Studios
www.hiddenart.com
Tel: 020 7729 3301

Houses of Parliament
www.parliament.uk
Tel: 020 7219 4272

Ironbridge Gorge Museum
www.ironbridge.org.uk
Tel: 01952 432 166

London Theatre Guide
By Metro Publications
Tel: 020 8533 0922 to order

National Trust
www.nationaltrust.org.uk
Tel: 0870 609 5380

Quince Honey Farm
www.quincehoney.co.uk
Tel: 01769 572401

Rock Factory Shops
www.handmadechocolates.co.uk
Tel: 01493 844676

Shakespeare's Globe
www.shakespeares-globe.org
Tel: 020 7401 9919

Theakstons
www.theakstons.co.uk
Tel: 01765 684 333

Youngs Brewery Tours
www.youngs.co.uk
020 8875 7005

Wensleydale Cheese
www.wensleydale.co.uk
Tel: 01969 667664

In theory at least, Italians make great lovers, the Swiss are efficient, French people are the best cooks and the English are eccentric. We all have our national stereotypes and if countless surveys among overseas visitors are to be believed, the comic character of Mr. Bean is fairly representative of the English. Our eccentricity is one of the aspects that attracts visitors and makes England such a special place to visit. And I think we're secretly rather proud of this tendency to mild lunacy.

Most of us content ourselves with just occasional flights of fantasy, the odd crazy suggestion to which others might reply, 'are you mad?'. Others have specific habits like old ladies who make a satisfying noise by running their walking sticks along railings, or my own personal favourite, skipping. Apparently 'proper grown ups' don't do it, and yet it's a great way to get anywhere, faster than walking but somehow more uplifting and less exhausting than running.

Some people have dedicated their life's work to being eccentric, often in such a way as to provide entertainment for others or create an obscure attraction in their own right. Rather than ridicule them, such people should be applauded. They attract valuable visitors from overseas and provide us with some great reasons to explore our own country and feel secretly pleased it's ours.

There are many museums where this kind of English eccentricity is celebrated. A lot of these are collections assembled by people with a single-minded interest in something the rest of us take for granted. There's the Lawnmower Museum in Southport with over 100 machines and even a Lavatory Museum in Staffordshire. If you looked forward to the start of a school term because it meant opening a smart box of new coloured pencils, then you'll probably love the Pencil Museum in Keswick. And if hot air's your thing, head for the Gas Museum in Leicester.

There are collections and museums of trinkets, gadgets and machines most of us rarely consider. Some cater for quite specialist tastes. How about the Pilchard Museum near Penzance or Norwich's Mustard Museum…

Some of the older members of the 'gentry' and upper classes are credited with leading the field in eccentricity. The legacy of earlier generations of aristocrats is a fairly strange selection of buildings which can be seen at locations through-out England. These have become part of our landscape, as accepted but not altogether rational landmarks. Anyone pointing out a strange building and asking anything about it is usually pacified with the somewhat glib response of 'it's a folly'. For some reason, the West Country seems to be particularly rich in them, glorying in wonderful mellow names like 'Burrow Mump' and 'Curry Rivel'. As well as having strange names and often very unlikely structures, the whole point of most follies is that they are pointless, or at least very odd.

Hadlow Folly in Kent is a 170ft fairy tale Gothic style tower. There are two popular local stories about its construction by Walter Barton May in the 1840's. It was either built to lure his wife back from the arms of a local farmer, or to enable Mr May to see the sea. What other reason could there be?

Lincoln not only boasts its beautiful Cathedral as a local land-mark, but also has an 'inland lighthouse' in the form of Dunstan Pillar. This was built by Sir Francis Dashwood, founder of the infamous 'Hell Fire Club' after a bet about whether a tall struc-ture with a small base could stand without falling over. He lost the bet so turned the tower into a lighthouse.

Many follies were built in remembrance of someone and are effectively glorified burial monuments. The Penshaw Hill monument near Durham resembles a Greek temple and was built in memory of the first Earl of Durham. Mortlake in Surrey is the unlikely setting for a full size Arab Sheik's Tent, built for the explorer Richard Burton.

Combe Martin in Devon has a more useful folly in the shape of a pub. The Pack of Cards Inn was built in 1626 by George Ley of Marwood, to celebrate a large win at cards. The inn has 52 windows — one for each card in the pack, and 4 floors — each with 13 doors. An entire tour of England could easily be conducted, using such follies as guiding posts and landmarks.

The English calendar is marked by various social occasions of varying levels of splendour. Some get excited about dressing for the Ascot Races or Henley Royal Regatta, whereas others like to get involved in lower profile and rather less predictable events. The organisers presumably regard their event as a perfectly natural fixture on the yearly calendar, but others could be forgiven for seeing them as slightly eccentric. Many have gained a world reputation and have taken place every year for several centuries.

The New Year gets off to a fine start with some great examples of English eccentricity. New Year's Day sees people across the country stripping off for a swim — outdoors in unheated waters. Whether these are the relative 'softies' taking a gentle dip in the Serpentine in London or the hardier ones (for some reason often over 70 years old…) wading into the North Sea at Whitley Bay, one would have expected the cold would bring them to their senses.

Others prefer to keep their feet a little closer to the ground but still indulge in not altogether sound activities. It isn't absolutely clear where the idea came from to hold a National Sedan Chair Carrying Competition every year in Lancaster but it appears to draw both participants and spectators as part of the Georgian Legacy Festival in late August. Around the same time, Bognor Regis on the South Coast attracts ambitious types with an interest in achieving impossible feats with its Birdman competition when serious and not so serious individuals try to 'fly' or jump a set distance off the end of the pier.

Costumes feature heavily through-out the year, sometimes as incidental to the events themselves and sometimes as a focal point. Scarecrow Festivals have suddenly become popular, but perhaps nowhere more so than in Kettlewell in the Yorkshire Dales when the supposedly scary, but often comic, effigies take over most of the village.

The English are not really known for their sporting prowess, but do seem to be fairly good at inventing completely new and mad sports or activities. Apart from reconfirming our status as the most eccentric country in Europe, this also has the benefit of ensuring that we become world champions at something.

A great example of this is the annual competition held in June each year at Ye Olde Royal Oak in Wetton in the Peak District – the World Toe Wrestling Championships. Apparently registered as an international sport, the game requires ankle power, ale and much cursing.

There are plenty of opportunities to join in these bizarre competitions. Should you wish to move to Ashbourne in Derbyshire, you'll automatically be in one of the teams (the Up'ards and Down'ards on opposite sides of the brook running through the village) for a mass football game which takes place every year on Shrove Tuesday and Ash Wednesday. Normal football rules don't quite apply as the goals are three miles apart and the ball specially made for the occasion out of leather and cork.

Apparently the World Conker Championships in Oundle near Peterborough first began over 30 years ago when a group of pub regulars tried to organise a fishing trip, were somehow thwarted and played conkers instead.

Those who are not now thinking that we are a 'bonkers' nation, will probably want to mark the first weekend in September in their diaries, when they'll have the opportunity to witness the World Black Pudding Throwing Championships held each year in Ramsbottom in Lancashire. The Black Puddings (blood sausages) are thrown at… 21 Yorkshire Puddings…

It's worth remaining in the North West for the next highlight of the social calendar with the Gurning Championships which is just one of the events included in the Egremont Crab Fair in Cumbria. This event has nothing to do with crabs but does include a chance for children to try to catch apples thrown from a cart. For the uninitiated, "gurning" means pulling incredible, and generally unattractive faces, for no particular reason.

Another essential event also takes place in Cumbria – the World's Biggest Liar competition is held annually in November at the Bridge Inn at Santon Bridge near Whitehaven. It dates back to the days when Will Ritson was a publican and kept his customers in the remote area of Wasdale entertained with tales of the area, including the information that the turnips in Wasdale were so big that after the locals had 'quarried' into them for Sunday Lunch they could be used as shelters by their sheep…

More Information:

Egremont Crab Fair and Gurning Championships
www.cumbria.uk.com

Follies
www.follies.btinternet.co.uk

Gas Museum
Tel: 0116 250 3190

Lancaster Tourism
www.lancaster.gov.uk
Tel: 01524 32878

Lavatory Museum in Staffordshire
Tel: 01543 490253

Lawnmower Museum
www.lawnmowerworld.co.uk
Tel: 01704 501336

Norwich's Mustard Museum
www.mustardshop.com
Tel: 01603/627889

Pencil Museum
www.pencils.co.uk
Tel: 017687 73626

Pilchard Museum
Tel: 01736 332112

Scarecrow Festival
www.kettlewell.info
Tel: 01756 760327

World Conker Championships
www.tom-and-ann.demon.co.uk/patch/conker.htm

World Toe Wrestling Championships
www.toewrestling.com

World's Biggest Liar Competition
www.copelandbc.gov.uk
Tel: 01946 852821

ENGLISH CALENDAR AND TRADITIONS

This is just a selection of events intended to give the essence of England rather than a comprehensive list. *www.whatsonwhen.com* is an excellent day-by-day calendar of many different types of events, festivals and happenings.

The following events have been chosen because they are particularly prominent markers throughout the year, represent centuries' old traditions, and are quirky or essential parts of the social calendar. These are all annual events which you can expect to find around the same time each year, although the precise dates may vary.

1st January – New Year's Day

Although it's really a Scottish tradition, First Footing is also popular in England. If the first person to cross the threshold of a house in the New Year is a tall dark man carrying coal, salt and a cake, you will have good luck through the year – consequently householders ask a suitably qualified individual to call round, and reward him with a good strong drink.

Another more healthy tradition is to 'blow away the cobwebs' and go for a good bracing walk to make up for the excesses of Christmas. The Ramblers' Association usually organise a programme of walks throughout the country.

5th January – Twelfth Night

This is traditionally the time when Christmas trees are taken down and it's considered bad luck to do so before this date. Being the end of the traditional Christmas season, in past times there was often a party with silly games managed by 'the Lord of Misrule'.

'Wassailing' also happened on Twelfth Night. Coming from the Anglo Saxon words 'Waes Heil', it means 'be whole' or healthy. People drank each other's health from a large wassail bowl, filled with a drink made of hot ale or cider, nutmeg, and sugar with roasted crab apples. In some parts of Britain, such as Herefordshire, trees and bees are still wassailed with a special song to ensure a healthy crop.

Mid January – Plough Monday

The first Monday after Twelfth Night was the day when farm work began again, often with spring ploughing. The plough was blessed (sometimes in church on the day before) and then dragged through the streets of the village. The tradition of Plough Monday still survives in some parts of Britain such as Nottinghamshire.

25th January – Burns Night

Another Scottish tradition is now creeping its way south, partly because of the migration of Scots' people and also because it provides a welcome break in the miserable month of January. It's the night when the birthday of Scots poet, Robert or 'Rabbie' Burns is celebrated.

The focal point of the feast is a haggis. This is made of minced mutton, offal, oatmeal and spices boiled in a sheep's stomach and tastes far better than it sounds. It's usually served with 'neaps and tatties' – a mixture of turnip, swede and potato, paraded before the dinner guests and serenaded by bagpipes, toasted with at least one 'wee dram' of whisky. Robert Burns' own words are used to 'address the haggis':

> "Fair fa' your honest sonsie face
> Great chieftain o' the pudden race…"

Mid February – Shrove Tuesday
(depends on Easter date)

Shrove Tuesday (from the old word 'shrive' meaning to confess) is the last day before Lent, when Christians are meant to give up their sins and ask forgiveness. They also decide on something which they will forego during the days of Lent. In the past, meat was not eaten during Lent.

Shrove Tuesday is also called Pancake Day when pancakes are made to use up rich foods before lent. Pancakes are incorporated into many village traditions and numerous pancake races held. This doesn't just mean getting to the finishing line, but also flipping a pre-cooked pancake in a frying pan a set number of times as you go and making sure the pancake is intact on arrival.

14th February – Valentine's Day

The origins of Valentine's Day supposedly go back to Roman times. In the past men and women put their names on slips of paper and drew lots as to who should be their love for the day. Nowadays the event is much more commercial, resulting in multi-million pound sales of flowers and cards...

7th-10th March – Crufts Dog Show

Known as a nation of animal-lovers, the English are particularly proud of their pooches, as demonstrated every year in Birmingham at the huge Crufts Dog Show.

Mid March – Mothering Sunday

Early Christians celebrated this festival on the fourth Sunday of Lent in honor of the Virgin Mary. In England, an ecclesiastical order expanded the holiday to include all mothers, and decreed it as Mothering Sunday. It later became a day when servants were allowed a day off to go and visit their mothers, often bringing a present such as a simnel cake.

March/April – Maundy Thursday
(depends on Easter date)

This is the last day of Lent. 'Maundy' means command and refers to when Jesus washed the feet of his disciples at the Last Supper and commanded his disciples to be humble and do likewise. Traditionally English kings and queens washed the feet of the poor and gave out gifts of clothing and food.

Nowadays the Queen seems to shy away from washing the feet of her citizens (the last Monarch to do this was James II). Instead she presents 'Maundy money' on Maundy Thursday each year at a different cathedral or abbey, to male and female pensioners from the local community, in recognition of their service to their community and their church. The number of recipients varies according to the monarch's age, increasing each year.

March/April – Good Friday
(depends on Easter date)

Although Easter is associated with Christianity, its beginnings go back to Anglo-Saxon times. 'Eostre' was the Anglo-Saxon goddess of the dawn and spring symbolising good luck and fertility. Because it is at the end of Winter and Lent, it has long been a time of celebration.

Before chocolate eggs were introduced, real eggs were decorated, symbolising Spring and new life. Various games and competitions take place, for example at Preston in Lancashire there is the custom of egg rolling. Hard boiled eggs are rolled down slopes to see whose egg goes furthest. In other places a game similar to conkers is played, in which one player's egg is

banged against an opponent's and the loser is the one whose egg breaks first. Another popular game for children is an egg hunt, finding eggs which have been hidden around the garden.

Children still enjoy making Easter bonnets (hats), decorated with practically anything that comes to hand. The custom is usually to include spring symbols such as daffodils, chickens, eggs and virtually anything yellow. This custom is part of the celebration of the end of Winter, a time when the winter wardrobe can be discarded, new clothes made and houses spring cleaned. Easter bonnet parades and competitions are held all over England.

March/April – Oxford and Cambridge Boat Race

This began in 1829 and now takes place every year, when one team each from the University of Oxford and Cambridge row from Putney to Mortlake near Richmond in London.

1st April – April Fools Day

This is the day to play tricks and practical jokes on people. If they fall for the joke they are April Fools – but only until midday because after that the joke is on you. Levels of inventiveness vary. A gullible tourist might be invited to watch the washing of the lions in Trafalgar Square in London. Even newspapers and television producers join in the game, usually planting a fictitious story to see if anyone spots it. Perhaps the most famous of these was in 1957 when the normally prim and proper Panorama television programme informed viewers that, even if money didn't grow on trees, spaghetti did. The BBC's switchboards were flooded with calls from people wanting to know where they could buy spaghetti bushes.

14th April – First Cuckoo Day

There is a custom that if you hear a cuckoo on this date you should turn over all the money in your pockets, spit and not look at the ground. If you do this and are standing on soft ground when you do it, you will have good luck but should you hear the cuckoo's call and do this when standing on hard ground, you'll only have bad luck.

Probably because the cuckoo is one of the birds whose arrival marks the start of spring and because its call is so distinctive, its arrival is well documented and eagerly awaited. Different areas even have dates when the cuckoo is expected – in Sussex on the 14th, Cheshire on the 15th, Worcestershire on the 20th and Yorkshire on 21st. There's even a tradition of reporting the first cuckoo in the letters' pages of the Times newspaper.

23rd April – St George's Day

This is as near as England comes to having a national day although the patron saint of St. George is shared with various other countries and he was actually from the Middle East! The English Tourism Council and various other organisations are now trying to stir up interest in St. George's Day and to encourage celebratory events. But you're still more likely to see the English flag (the red cross of St. George on a white background) flying when the English football team is playing.

1st May – May Day

Traditionally a day of great merry-making, with celebrations including dancing around a maypole, Morris dancing and the election and parading of a May Queen.

Beginning of May – International Dawn Chorus Day

This annual event is organised by the Wildlife Trust, normally on the first Sunday in May. All around the country (and world) birdwatchers are invited to arrange an early morning gathering, just before dawn, to witness the Dawn Chorus and celebrate one of nature's miracles.

Early May – Furry Dance

Helston in Cornwall is the focal point for a traditional celebration dating back to pagan times. Couples dance through the streets in formal dress through-out the day, bringing good luck to the houses of the town. The dance always take place on the 8th of May (except when this falls on a Sunday or Monday when the dance is held on the previous Saturday).

Early May – Punch's Birthday

Punch and Judy are traditional puppets which are celebrated on the Saturday nearest to 9th May at St. Paul's Church in Covent Garden. Punch and Judy "professors" (the puppeteers) assemble in the church to hear a sermon by a puppet. Outside the church there are many free Punch and Judy shows for children.

Mid May – Chelsea Flower Show

The grounds of the Chelsea Royal Hospital (famous for its soldier pensioners in smart red uniforms) are transformed by the Royal Horticultural Society for a week every year for this gardening show with a world wide reputation. Tickets are sold out well in advance so apply early.

131

29th May – Oak Apple Day

Oak Apple Day celebrates the time when the then future King Charles II escaped his roundhead enemies by hiding in an oak tree. Sprigs of oak leaves are traditionally worn in memory of the king's lucky escape. In the small Derbyshire town of Castleton, this celebration is combined with an ancient fertility rite and called Garland Day. A garlanded king and queen parade the town and there is Morris dancing and other merriment.

Early June – Appleby Horse Fair

Thousands of travellers and other visitors arrive in Appleby in Cumbria for a week of trading and racing horses and generally enjoying themselves. The horse fair has been held since the 17th century and is a very lively event – some horses change hands several times during the fair.

10th June – Trooping the Colour

This is the Queen's official birthday, marked by a special procession at Horse Guards' Parade, London. One of the five regiments of Foot Guards assembles at the parade ground, where they march to the music of massed military bands. Then a guardsman carries the flag, or colour, of the regiment along the ranks. The custom began to ensure that all the soldiers could recognize their own flag in battle. Now it is one of the main royal ceremonies and a draw to tourists from all over the world.

12th June – The Dunmow Flitch

Every leap year, happily married couples in the village of
Dunmow in Essex have the opportunity to win an entire side
(or flitch) of bacon if they can prove that they have never had
an argument.... Not many couples win.

Mid June – Royal Ascot

The horses often take second place during this four day world-
class horse-racing event, especially on Ladies Day when
women vie with each other to wear the smartest outfits and
biggest hats. The attendance of the Queen and other members
of the Royal Family in the Royal Enclosure also draws
celebrity watchers. It is almost impossible to get into the
Royal Enclosure but you can get tickets to be part of the
general fashion frolics.

21st June – Summer Solstice

This is the day when the sun is at its highest in the sky. The
most famous celebration of the Summer Solstice is at the stone
circle at Stonehenge when white-robed Druids gather to
watch the sun rising over the Heel Stone, one of the stones
that lies outside the main circle at Stonehenge.

Early July – Henley Royal Regatta

Hundreds of teams compete in this rowing regatta on the
River Thames about an hour from London. Socialising, seeing
and being seen is just as important in the various enclosures.
Dress codes are usually strict, with men often wearing a boater
hat, although many people choose to enjoy the spectacle in
more relaxed mode by picnicking on the banks of the Thames.

15th July – St Swithin's Day

According to tradition, if it rains on St Swithin's Day, it will rain for the next 40 days. The story began in the year 971, when the bones of St Swithin who died around 870 were moved to a special shrine at Winchester Cathedral. A storm began which reportedly lasted for 40 days and it was said that St. Swithin was weeping in heaven because his bones had been disturbed.

Third week of July – Swan-upping

This curious ceremony involves the capture of the swans on the Thames to mark their beaks according to their owners. Most of the swans belong to the Queen except for those owned by two Livery Companies, the Dyers and Vintners. "Upping" means turning the birds upside-down, to mark the birds or check whether their beaks are marked. When this task is completed a banquet is held – featuring roast swan.

End of July – Oyster season

Whitstable in Kent is famous for its excellent oysters so when the oyster season begins on the first Thursday after the 25th July the oyster-fishing boats are blessed.

Beginning of August – Cowes Week

This one week regatta takes place on the Isle of Wight and every level of sailor can take part. Part of the fun of Cowes Week is not just the sailing but also the parties, balls and other private functions.

Mid September – Last Night of the Proms

The BBC Henry Wood Promenade Concert season starts in mid July and runs until the famous last night in September and takes place in the Royal Albert Hall in London. Founded in 1895 the Proms were intended to entertain people who stayed in London during the Summer and to promote new music and musicians. The Last Night is a fun event and was originally when people who spent the Summer in their second homes in the country returned to London and met their friends.

4th–6th October – Nottingham Goose Fair

Called the Goose Fair from the days when geese were driven into the town for sale, this is Britain's biggest fair and now over 700 years old. It includes over 150 rides, 450 games and food from around the world.

Beginning of October – Pearly King Harvest Festival

London's market stall holders are called costermongers and since the last century some of the leading costermongers have been "pearly kings and queens". The name comes from the mother of pearl buttons which cover their suits. The titles are passed on through families and they undertake various fundraising activities. On the first Sunday in October they hold a harvest festival in the church of St Martin-in-the-Fields, London.

31st October – Halloween or All Hallows' Eve

This tradition goes back to the Celts who believed that the boundary between the dead and living merged on this night.

Nowadays it is celebrated in a fun way, mainly by children who hollow out pumpkins to make lanterns, play apple-bobbing and dress up as ghosts and ghouls.

3rd November – The London to Brighton Veteran Car Run

This annual event commemorates the "Emancipation Run" when a new act was passed increasing the speed limit from four miles per hour to 14 and abolishing the need for a man to precede cars carrying a red flag (the latter was actually abolished in 1878 but a red flag was symbolically destroyed at the start of the 1896 run). Around 350 cars built before 1905 leave Hyde Park in central London and finish in Brighton.

5th November – Bonfire Night

Every English school child is taught the story of the failed Gunpowder Plot by Guy Fawkes who tried to blow up the Houses of Parliament. Almost every town and village holds a bonfire night with fireworks and a stuffed effigy of Guy Fawkes on top of the bonfire.

1st December – first day of Advent

As well as advent services in churches, advent candles (marked with the 24 days before Christmas and lit each day so by Christmas Day the candle is burnt down) and advent calendars are used by children in the countdown to Christmas.

December – The Preparation for Christmas

Around this time preparations begin in earnest in most primary schools and Christian churches for a Nativity Play re-enacting the birth of Jesus Christ to which parents are invited.

December is also the time of year when theatres put on pantomimes which are usually major sell-outs. Based on fairy tales (e.g. Cinderella and Snow White) and often featuring TV stars, they are humorous plays for children which adults also enjoy. The main male and female roles are usually reversed so the lead female is played by a man and vice versa. Audience participation is encouraged with lots of shouting and interaction between the audience and actors, especially "oh no, s/he isn't", "oh yes, s/he is" repeated several times.

In the lead up to Christmas shops, houses, pubs and other public places are decorated. Holly and Ivy and the colours red, green and gold are very popular. Streets are illuminated with colourful lights strung across the road.

Most houses have a Christmas Tree of some sort – either a fir tree or artificial version. These were first introduced in 1841 when Prince Albert brought one from Germany. Since the Second World War a huge Christmas Tree has been donated by the people of Norway and erected in Trafalgar Square.

Most people also send Christmas cards to each other, increasingly buying cards which include a donation to charity. Charity collections are also made by carol singers.

24th December – Christmas Eve

Christians go to a special service at their church on Christmas Eve night, often candle-lit. Children become overexcited, waiting for the arrival of "Father Christmas" who supposedly comes while they are asleep. Many leave out mince pies and brandy for him, and perhaps a carrot or some food for his reindeers. They hang up stockings, bags and pillow cases in the expectation that if they have been well behaved they'll receive lots of presents.

25th December – Christmas Day

This is the focal point for most Christmas celebrations, marked with present-giving, visiting friends and relatives, possibly going to church but almost certainly with the twin tradition of Christmas Dinner and "listening to the Queen".

Christmas dinner includes turkey, vegetables (especially sprouts and chestnuts), stuffing, cranberry sauce and gravy, followed by Christmas pudding and perhaps mince pies. Regardless of whether they are normally interested in the Royal Family or not, it's a tradition to watch or listen to the Queen's Christmas Message at three o'clock in the afternoon.

26th December – Boxing Day

Like Christmas Day this is always a national holiday. The name comes from "boxing up" presents for servants and it being the day that alms boxes at churches were opened and distributed to the poor. Sports matches are often popular on Boxing Day. It's also when mad or very brave people swim in the Serpentine in Hyde Park in London.

31st December – New Year's Eve

Party time!

WAYS TO ENJOY ENGLAND

There are times when you want to explore specific areas of the country or go on a certain sort of short break such as a relaxing holiday by the sea, and others when you just want to "do something". Here's a collection of suggested ways to simply enjoy England…

❖ Think you know an area really well? No matter, how well you know a place, there's always something new to learn. Join a tour, follow a trail or choose a theme – the first place to go before you explore a new town or area is the Tourist Information Centre where you'll find armfuls of brochures and lots of local knowledge. There's a full list of over 500 TICs on the website – *www.travelengland.org.uk*.

❖ Walk the Thames – it flows for 147 miles outside London from its trickling source in the Cotswold Hills past Oxford, Henley, Windsor Castle and Hampton Court Palace to London. The Thames Path is well-signposted so you can start walking or boating at any point along it, or enjoy one of the 300 annual events and regattas which take place along the Thames. The Thames Path is now the longest riverwalk in Europe, running for 175 miles in all – *www.visitthames.co.uk*.

❖ See a different version of England, visiting places that are bound to stick in your memory – Great Cockup, Macaroni Wood, Amen Corner and Ugley would do as a start. To do this you'll need the "Hysterical Mappe of Britain", which costs £8.99 from Birdlip Maps (*Tel: 020 7376 4549*) who have produced a special map focusing on 500 unusual and strange place names.

❖ Stay in a real castle, complete with a portcullis which is lowered each night. Amberley Castle is 900 years' old in 2003 – a midweek stay is slightly cheaper than a weekend one – *www.AmberleyCastle.co.uk*.

❖   Experience an old-fashioned and ever so slightly "tacky" day out at Blackpool Pleasure Beach with its golden mile of gaudy amusement arcades, over 140 rides and the night-time illuminations. You'll either love it (some people obviously do, it's one of Britain's most visited attractions) or hate it – *www.blackpooltourism.com*.

❖   Stay somewhere guaranteed to be different. "Historic Farmhouses in Cumbria" have 11 properties with plenty of character, unusual architectural features and lots of history. Choose from a 17th century house with no mains electricity and water from only a local spring, the most remote country house in England and a medieval mansion – *www.historicfarm-snw.co.uk*.

❖   Enjoy a balmy summer evening, first-class entertainment and the beautiful setting of a stately home. There are open-air concerts in some of England's finest historic houses and castles such as Blenheim Palace, Burghley and Harewood House, often with fireworks to finish – *www.performingarts.co.uk*.

❖   One of the things which often surprise new visitors to London are its green spaces and parks. "The Green-Spaces Guide to London" gives details of all the well-known ones as well as hidden treasures such as the Chelsea Physic Garden and the Geffrye Museum's herb garden – see if you can manage to visit all 150 of them – *www.green-spaces.co.uk*.

❖   Well dressing is an ancient practice when wells and springs are decorated with pictures made from flower petals, seeds and leaves and then blessed. It's a custom most associated with the Peak District where there are around 80 well dressings every Summer, often used as the basis for other village festivals. Following a trail of well dressings is a pleasant way to spend a day, especially as many of the villages are set in beautiful countryside – *www.welldressing.com*.

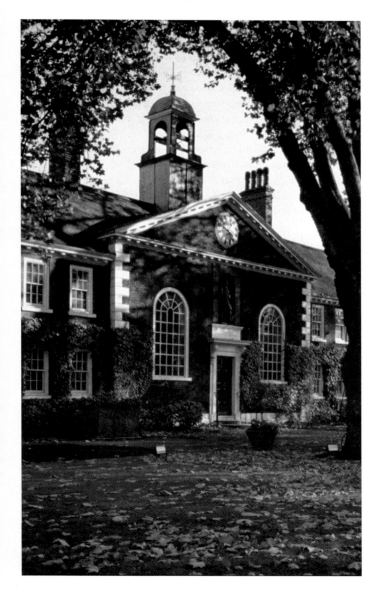

❖ Enjoy a holiday afloat, combining travel and accommodation. There are 3000 miles of canals and rivers to choose from in Britain. You can hire whatever craft you prefer from cruiser to traditional narrowboat, sleeping from two to ten people. Visit *www.waterwayholidaysuk.com* or obtain the "Waterways Holidays UK" brochure free from British Tourist Authority offices or by telephoning *08702 415956.*

❖ Pubs – an essential part of English life. If you fancy exploring a new area but think you'll need some liquid refreshments along the way, there are many books outlining pub walks as well as websites like *www.classicpubwalks.com* which combine history with enjoyment of the local brew.

❖ You don't need to dress up for one of England's most "casual" events – the annual Scarecrow Festival in August at Kettlewell near Skipton in North Yorkshire features over 100 scarecrows. They are hidden around the village and in the past have featured a vicar, bride, fishermen, chimney sweep, babies and a clown. There are trails and quizzes for children and adults as well as refreshment stops featuring home-baking and the Blue Bell Inn dating back to 1680 – *www.kettlewell.info.*

❖ What could be more English than displays of plants, show gardens, cream teas and summer music played on the bandstand? Chelsea Flower Show incorporates all these and is one of the highlights in an English gardener's year, taking place every May. You'll need to book early – but if you miss Chelsea, the Royal Horticultural Society also organises shows at Hampton Court Palace and Tatton Park in Cheshire – *www.rhs.org.uk.*

❖ English people are considered thoroughly eccentric. Why not plan a tour of follies, visiting crazy people, unusual events and bizarre buildings. The Eccentric Guide to Britain (there's also one focusing on just London) by Benedict le Vay provides an ideal travel companion – *www.bradt-travelguides.com*.

❖ Plan a tour of England, focusing on regional specialities. There are now over 400 varieties of British cheese so there'll almost always be a local cheese to find. Eat Kippers in Northumbria, Yorkshire Pudding in Yorkshire, Bakewell Pudding in Bakewell, Melton Mowbray Pie in the Midlands, a cream tea in Devon, Cornish Pasties in Cornwall and asparagus in Evesham – *www.travelengland.org.uk*.

❖ Hop-on, hop-off – on a tour bus. Companies like Guide Friday have an ever-increasing range of tours in towns and cities, some well-known like York or Stratford-upon-Avon, others lesser known like Leicester which has the new National Space Centre to visit. The best thing about this type of tour is that you can use it to get a basic orientation and then simply get off when you see something you want to visit, joining the tour at the same place later in the day – *www.guidefriday.com*.

❖ For a tour with a difference, take a trip around a cemetery. Whether you want to trace your ancestors, look out for intriguing inscriptions on headstones or discover more about a local area, cemeteries are often beautiful, even amusing places to visit. Two of the best known ones are St. James at Highgate in north London *www.tales.ndirect.co.uk* and Kensal Green in London *www.rbkc.gov.uk* where tours are offered, featuring gravestones of the famous and infamous.

❖ English Heritage's programme of historical re-enactments really make history come alive. Featuring craft demonstrations, fierce battles, pageantry, period music and royal visits, the events are set in ruins, gardens, houses, castles and abbeys and take place all around the country throughout the summer months – *www.english-heritage.org.uk*.

❖ There has never been a shortage of places to walk and enjoy the English countryside but now there are even more routes to ramble, thanks to the introduction of a new network of national trails. The Ramblers Association aim to help everyone enjoy walking outdoors and their website includes urban as well as countryside walks, publications, maps and even chances to find walking companions so no excuses for not setting off right now! – *www.ramblers.org.uk*

❖ With such huge swathes of open land, it's perhaps surprising that Britain's biggest walking festival takes place not on the mainland but on the much smaller Isle of Wight. The annual festival includes about 80 walks themed and categorised from easy to strenuous. You can learn about the island's history as you walk, looking for dinosaur footprints or Queen Victoria's favourite retreat – *www.islandbreaks.co.uk*.

❖ London isn't an obvious place to go to enjoy a countryside walk. Mention an orbital route and most people are more likely to think of the M25 than a footpath. The London Loop is a 150 mile scenic circuit of Greater London, with 24 sections mainly connected to public transport and featuring walks along rivers and canals, with many peaceful wildlife havens along the way – *www.londonwalking.com*.

❖ With so many attractions to visit in major cities such as London, Bath and York, costs can get pretty high. Leisure Pass help to reduce the bill by providing smart cards which, once bought, then provide free entry to a wide range of attractions as well as discounted car rental, theatre tickets and free tours – *www.yorkpass.com, www.bathpass.com* and *www.londonpass.com*.

❖ Whether you enjoy great literature or comedy, classical or world music, pop or jazz, over 100 arts festivals take place in Britain every year. Some of them are long-established international events such as the Hay-on-Wye Literature Festival *www.hayfestival.co.uk* and others newer lesser-known events. The British Arts Festival Association provides examples of them on their web site – *www.artsfestivals.co.uk*.

❖   England's many museums are veritable "Palaces of Discovery" and a large percentage of them are free to visit including the Imperial War, Natural History, Science, National Maritime, and British Museums, Tate, National and National Portrait Galleries in London, Manchester's Museum of Science and Industry, York's National Railway Museum and the National Museums and Galleries on Merseyside. The national website has a growing database of 2500 museums, galleries and heritage attractions and details of Museums and Galleries Month – *www.24hourmuseum.org.uk*.

❖   The National Trust is well-known for preserving and maintaining historic houses and opening them up to the public. This prominent charity is also one of the largest landowners in England, with massive areas of the coast and countryside which are open to the public, as well as offering gardens to visit, a full programme of events, behind the scenes tours, cottages to rent and properties to hire for special events – *www.nationaltrust.org.uk*.

❖   Every September around 2500 buildings which are usually private open their doors to the public, often for free. Heritage Open Days and the London Open House event are massively popular, usually prompting queues at the most popular venues as the public seize the chance to look inside local landmarks, curious conversions and ancient buildings – *www.londonopen-house.org* and *www.civictrust.org.uk*.

❖   It's worth looking out for special openings and events which give a different view and insight into some of England's best known attractions. During the winter months, visitors can step back into the atmospheric past with an evening lantern-light tour of Hampton Court Palace led by a guide in

Stuart costume. The Ceremony of the Keys has taken place for centuries every evening at the Tower of London. Visitors are welcome although you need to book in advance to witness this ancient custom – *www.hrp.org.uk*.

❖ One of the best ways of understanding the past is to re-live it. Open air museums like Beamish and Ironbridge cover several acres and visiting them really does feel like escaping the modern world. Beamish features a period tram and bus transport, colliery, village, farm, turn-of-the-century shops, pubs and houses. Ironbridge has the famous bridge as well as canals, factories, furnaces and workshops – *www.beamish.org.uk* and *www.ironbridge.org.uk*.

❖ Most people recognise well-known landmarks like Tower Bridge in London (although they often call it London Bridge which is very different) and yet how many have ever been inside this famous icon, seen the Thames from high above on the covered walkways or got an insight into how the Victorian machines make it lift to admit ships? – *www.towerbridge.org.uk*

❖ Despite being noisy, bumpy and old-fashioned there was a public outcry when plans were announced to get rid of the traditional red double-decker London Routemaster buses with an open platform at the rear. Now plans have been announced to keep the 600 still in service and introduce another 24 which have been refurbished to be more efficient and environmentally friendly. They're a great, good value way to see London's main sights – routes 11, 15 and 24 are highly recommended – *www.londontransport.co.uk*.

❖ The film Notting Hill made London garden squares even more famous. Often locked and only accessible to the wealthy individuals who live in the houses around the squares, they are frequently large, green spaces with hidden corners, mini woodlands and imaginative planting. London Garden

Squares Day is now an annual event on the second Sunday in June, when they open to the public (*Tel: 0870 3331183*).

❖ Royal Ascot, Chelsea Flower Show and the Proms at the Royal Albert Hall are the epitomy of the English social calendar. It's possible to join in all of them so book early, dress in your finest clothes and experience them all first-hand – *www.whatsonwhen.com*.

❖ The Lawn Tennis Championships at Wimbledon attract a world-wide following and tickets for Centre Court are allocated mainly by ballot at the beginning of every year. It's still possible to go along and experience the fun atmosphere (even when it rains), eat strawberries and cream and even enjoy some tennis on the other courts. All you need to do is join the queue (this is part of the fun) early in the morning on the day of play for a Ground Admission ticket – *www.wimbledon.org*.

❖ At the beginning of May, English woodlands are at their best, with the new deciduous buds open and fresh, birds singing and a carpet of bluebells under foot. You can find a woodland to walk in and even plant and dedicate a tree to someone by visiting the Woodland Trust website – *www.woodlandtrust.org.uk*.

❖ There's nothing quite so harmless and yet which feels so self-indulgent as a really good afternoon tea, in a fine hotel or a small cosy tea shop. Linger and natter as long as you can, there are great suggestions for places on – *www.gofortea.com*.

❖ England's weather isn't quite as sunny as the Mediterranean but nor is the South of France quite so blessed as the English coast with craggy seaside resorts and rock pools. Put on your wellies (or ignore your crinkled, cold toes) and pretend you're a child again, searching for beautiful shells, crabs and other sea treasures beside the sea. Go to old-fashioned resorts like Lyme Regis for a taste of the past and chance to find a fossil – *www.lymeregis.com*.

❖ Ever been to a place for the first time but thought it looked familiar? It might be because of one of your past lives, or more likely that it is a film location. Follow in the footsteps of the famous by seeking out film locations. The British Tourist Authority publishes a "movie-map" to show you where they are – *www.visitbritain.com*.

❖ England has some fantastic gardens, very different from each other. Beth Chatto deliberately planted a garden in Essex *www.bethchatto.co.uk* which doesn't need watering, the Lost Gardens of Heligan in Cornwall *www.heligan.com* have now been rediscovered, Great Dixter in Sussex *www.greatdixter.co.uk* is constantly changing and experimenting with new colour schemes and structures, and Haddon Hall in the Peak

District has one of the most romantic gardens in the country – *www.haddonhall.co.uk*. There is a garden finder on *www.visitbritain.com*.

❖ Those who don't understand the appeal of bitter can't get to grips with the idea of not serving all beer ice cold. Whether you're one of these or already convinced, CAMRA (Campaign for Real Ale) can help you gain an insight into the great English institution of pubs – and suggest many beer festivals to attend for an in-depth understanding of the subject – *www.camra.org.uk*.

❖ Mention stone circles and everyone immediately thinks of Stonehenge – but two other lesser-known ones are worth visiting too. Avebury is close to Stonehenge in Wiltshire (don't miss the nearby Stones restaurant) and Castlerigg in the Lake District – *www.visitwiltshire.co.uk* and *www.cumbria.com*.

❖ When you feel you really know England and want another adventure, why not go to one of the islands – Isle of Man *www.gov.im/tourism* and Lindisfarne *www.lindisfarne.org.uk* in the North, Isle of Wight *www.isle-of-wight-tourism.gov.uk*, Burgh Island *www.burghisland.com*, Lundy *www.lundyisland.co.uk*, and the Scilly Isles *www.scillyonline.co.uk* in the South.

❖ If you're travelling around England, experiencing varied types of accommodation can give you fresh perspectives and different insights. Why not go on a tour, staying in progressively better places as you go – camping, bed and breakfast (in a cottage and then a castle), small guesthouse, even a country house hotel.

❖ Eat your way around the world – in England. Thanks to many different communities you can find restaurants reflecting almost any of the world's great cuisines – French, Italian, Thai, Chinese, Indian, Vietnamese…

❖ Enjoy agriculture at its finest, by visiting one of the major county shows when livestock of every description are groomed and paraded, crafts demonstrated and food sampled. Most take place between May and July – choose from the South Suffolk, Devon County, Royal Bath and West, Surrey County, Royal Cornwall, Three Counties, Shropshire and West Midland, and the Royal Shows – *www.whatsonwhen.com*.

YOU DON'T KNOW
LONDON UNLESS
YOU'VE...

No matter how many times you've visited London or how long you've lived there, guaranteed there are plenty of places you've still not seen. Some of them hidden, others well-known but still on the "one day" list. You can't be said to really know London unless you've…

- Joined in a tour with a Yeoman Warder "Beafeater" at the Tower of London.

- Gone to grab an antique bargain at 6.00 am from Bermondsey market.

- Flown a kite on Hampstead Heath and enjoyed home made food in the Brew House Café at Kenwood House.

- Seen Tower Bridge from the inside, crossing the river through the walkways.

- Thrown your voice in the Whispering Gallery at St. Paul's Cathedral.

- Bought plants and flowers on a Sunday morning at Columbia Road Flower Market.

- Eaten strawberries and cream at the Centre Court café at the Wimbledon Lawn Tennis Museum.

- Seen the beautiful view (protected by an act of parliament) from Richmond Hill.

- Watched a performance at Shakespeare's Globe.

- Walked along the South Bank of the Thames from the Design Museum to Waterloo Bridge.

- Met a World War II bus conductor at London's Transport Museum.

- Shopped at Covent Garden and watched the buskers.

- Been on a river cruise and seen London's famous sights from the Thames.

- Shopped in one of London's ethnic areas like Green Street, Newham and eaten a curry in Brick Lane.

- Seen the giant Amazonian water lily in the Princess of Wales' conservatory, Kew Gardens.

- Seen Botticelli's Venus & Mars and Van Gogh's Chair at the National Gallery.

- Got lost in the maze at Hampton Court Palace.

- Visited one of London's lesser known museums like the Old Operating Theatre Museum and Herb Garret.

LOOK AT LONDON – WHERE TO GO TO GET A GREAT VIEW...

- Wellington Arch, Hyde Park Corner – go inside this majestic landmark for a stunning view across the surrounding parks and as far away as the Houses of Parliament.

- See a sight you've often seen on television for real – visit Centre Court during a tour of the Wimbledon Lawn Tennis Museum.

- See London's famous sights from a different perspective – from the River Thames with a City Cruises' sightseeing trip.

- Look down on the River Thames and some of London's new landmarks like the London Eye from Tower Bridge's covered walkways.

- See magnificent new architecture and old dockers' houses from the vantage point of the Docklands Light Railway.

- Feast your eyes on the structure of the stage and building at Shakespeare's Globe as well as enjoying the performances. You can learn more by taking a back-stage tour or visiting the exhibition.

- On a clear day amaze yourself with the view from the top of Henry VIII's mound in Richmond Park – an uninterrupted view across London to St Paul's Cathedral.

- Walk in the footsteps of former prisoners at the Tower of London, from Traitor's Gate to the execution site on Tower Hill.

- Climb the Monument for an old fashioned view of the Pool of London.

- From the Ridgeway in Enfield you can see all the way southwards to Canary Wharf.

- If you can get a table at the Oxo Tower, you will be rewarded with stunning sunsets over London.

- Sir Christopher Wren said the view from Islands Gardens at the tip of the Isle of Dogs across the river was 'the best view in Europe'. From here you can gaze across the water to Wren's Royal naval College and the Old Royal Observatory. You can watch the Timeball fall at 1300 hours and set your watch to Greenwich Mean Time. Likewise the view from the Royal Observatory is a spectacular one.

FOOD FOR THE SOUL

Fed up of over-priced cavernous designer restaurants? Feed your mind and lift your spirit with a snack or feast…

- Did you know you can enjoy lunch, tea or dinner as you cruise past along the Thames? The London Showboat also includes entertainment and songs from the West End Shows.

- Eat Al Fresco even when the sun doesn't shine – at Covent Garden Market where you'll also be entertained by buskers and opera singers.

- Work up an appetite with a wander through the gardens at Kew and then enjoy a meal in one of the cafés or restaurants.

- Eat and relax in the Orangery built for Queen Anne at Kensington Palace.

- For a feeling of peace, enjoy the historic setting of the Crypt Café in St. Paul's Cathedral.

- Buy your own fruit, meat and vegetables fresh from the farmer at Borough Market.

- The Brew House Café at Kenwood is particularly well-known for its hearty breakfast – worth getting-up for…

- How about a picnic in a park? There are plenty of green spaces throughout London – in Richmond, Enfield, Lee Valley Regional Park, Sutton, and Mile End Park.

- Try a cold-cure with a difference – a curry in one of the myriad of restaurants in Brick Lane, London E1. Hot food's also supposed to keep your heart healthy…

- Wine's usually an accompaniment to a meal but at Vinopolis it's the star – try a gourmet meal at the award-winning Cantina Vinopolis.

- Eat lunch at the Royal Festival Hall and you'll be able to enjoy their free foyer events at the same time.

- You can't eat there but it might give you some ideas or make you grateful for your modern cooker – feast your eyes on the way we cooked in Tudor times in the kitchens at Hampton Court Palace.

BREATHING – WALKS & OUTDOOR ACTIVITIES

Most people think of London as an over-populated town but it's also full of beautiful green spaces, and places to walk and explore. Here are some suggested ways to enjoy them…

- Visit one of London's green boroughs and explore the countryside close to the city – try Enfield, Sutton, and Richmond.

- Explore over 300 acres and discover more than 30,000 different types of plant at the Royal Botanic Gardens, Kew.

- Spot red and fallow deer in Richmond Park, descended from the herds of Henry VIII's time and picnic under oaks that are over 400 years old.

- Stroll across the 25 metre wide Green Bridge in Mile End Park, designed by award winning architect Piers Gough.

- Discover more about Darwinism at Down House, now protected and opened to the public by English Heritage or relax on the Kenwood Estate by Kenwood House.

- Spot the statues, obelisks and winding lake in the Italianate Gardens of Chiswick House.

- Dip into the murky world of pond creatures and learn about bugs and other wildlife at the Sutton Ecology Centre.

- Pretend you're preparing for a life on the ocean waves, with a trip on the Thames with City Cruises, enjoying the view from Westminster to Greenwich.

- Lose yourself (or your children!) in the maze at Hampton Court Palace or explore the six acres of interiors with one of the Palace's costumed guides.

APPENDIX

USEFUL ORGANISATIONS & WEBSITES

Tourist Boards

Cumbria Tourist Board
⌨ *Ashleigh, Holly Road, Windermere, Cumbria, LA23 2AQ*
☎ *015394 44444*
✎ *www.golakes.co.uk*
Covering Cumbria and The Lake District.

East Of England Tourist Board
⌨ *Toppesfield Hall, Hadleigh, Suffolk, IP7 5DN*
☎ *01473 822922*
✎ *www.eastofenglandtouristboard.com*
Covering Cambridgeshire, Essex Hertfordshire, Bedfordshire,
Norfolk, and Suffolk.

Heart Of England Tourist Board
⌨ *Larkhill Road, Worcester, WR5 2EF*
☎ *01905 763436*
✎ *www.visitheartofengland.com*
Covering Derbyshire, Gloucestershire, Leicestershire,
Lincolnshire, Northamptonshire, Nottinghamshire, Shropshire,
Staffordshire, Warwickshire, Hereford, Worcester, and the West
Midlands.

London Tourist Board
⌨ *1 Warwick Row, London, SW1P 5ER*
☎ *020 7932 2000*
✎ *www.londontouristboard.com*
Covering Greater London.

Northumbria Tourist Board

⊡ *Aykley Heads, Durham, DH1 5UX*

☎ *020 0191 375 3000*

✎ *www.visitnorthumbria.com*

Covering Durham, Northumberland, the Tees Valley, and Tyne and Wear.

North West Tourist Board

⊡ *Swan House, Swan Meadow Road,*
Wigan Pier, Wigan, WN3 5BB

☎ *01942 821222*

✎ *www.visitnorthwest.com*

Covering Cheshire, Greater Manchester, Lancashire, Merseyside.

South East Of England Tourist Board

⊡ *The Old Brew House,*
Warwick Park, Tunbridge Wells, Kent, TN2 5TU

☎ *01892 540766*

✎ *www.southeastengland.uk.com and www.gosouth.co.uk*

Covering Sussex, Kent, and Surrey.

Southern Tourist Board

⊡ *40 Chamberlayne Road, Eastleigh, Hampshire, SO50 5JH*

☎ *023 8062 5400*

✎ *www.gosouth.co.uk*

Covering Berkshire, East Dorset, Hampshire, Isle of Wight, Buckinghamshire, and Oxfordshire.

South West Tourism

⊡ *Woodwater Park, Pynes Hill, Exeter, EX2 5WT*

☎ *0870 442 0830*

✎ *www.westcountrynow.com*

Covering Bath, Bristol, Cornwall and the Isles of Scilly, Devon, West Dorset, Somerset, and Wiltshire.

Yorkshire Tourist Board

▣ *312 Tadcaster Road, York, YO24 1GS*

☎ *01904 707961*

✎ *www.yorkshirevisitor.com*

Covering Yorkshire, North Lincolnshire, and North East Lincolnshire.

British Tourist Authority

▣ *Thames Tower, Black's Road,*
  Hammersmith, London, W6 9EL

☎ *020 8846 9000*

✎ *www.visitbritain.com*

Responsible for the promotion of England, Scotland, Wales, and Northern Ireland.

Tourist Information Centres

England has a national network of over 500 Tourist Information Centres (TICS). The Centres all perform to a national standard and offer accommodation bookings, information on places to visit, transport options and a wide range of guide books. A full list of TICs can be seen on *www.TravelEngland.org.uk*.

Accessibility

Holiday Care

▣ *Imperial Buildings, Victoria Road,*
  Horley, Surrey, RH6 7PZ

☎ *01293 771500   Minicom: 01293 776943*

✎ *www.holidaycare.org.uk*

Holiday Care is the UK`s central source of travel and holiday information for disabled people, older people and carers. They have a computerised database with information about accessible tourist facilities in the UK and overseas.

RADAR (Royal Association for Disability and Rehabilitation)

⌨ *12 City Forum, 250 City Road, London, EC1V 8AF*

☎ *020 7250 3222 Minicom: 020 7250 4119*

✍ *www.radar.org.uk*

Information line providing advice with over 80 booklets and fact sheets available.

Heritage

English Heritage

⌨ *23 Savile Row, London, W1X 1AB*

☎ *020 7973 3000*

✍ *www.english-heritage.org.uk*

Manage, conserve and market over 400 ancient and historic properties.

Historic Houses Association

⌨ *2 Chester Street, London, SW1X 7BB*

☎ *020 7259 5688*

✍ *www.hha.org.uk*

Provides advice, liaison and services to historic country houses and gardens in private ownership in the UK, approximately 300 of which are open to the public on a regular basis.

Landmark Trust

⌨ *Shottesbrooke, Maidenhead, Berkshire, SL6 3SW*

☎ *01628 825925*

✍ *www.landmarktrust.co.uk*

Rescues and restores architecturally interesting and historic buildings at risk, giving them renewed life by letting them for self-catering holidays.

The Civic Trust

🖂 *17 Carlton House Terrace, London, SW1Y 5AW*

☎ *020 7930 0914*

✎ *www.civictrust.org.uk*

Undertakes regeneration projects, campaigns and promotes Heritage Open Days.

The National Trust

🖂 *36 Queen Anne`s Gate, London, SW1H 9AS*

☎ *020 7222 9251*

✎ *www.nationaltrust.org.uk*

Cares for 200 historic houses, 230 gardens & landscape parks, 600 miles of coast, and 612,000 acres of open countryside.

Campaign for Museums

🖂 *Grosvenor Gardens House,*
35-37 Grosvenor Gardens,
London, SW1W 0BX

☎ *020 7233 9796*

✎ *www.24hourmuseum.org.uk*

Manages annual Museums Week, Museums and Galleries Month in May each year and the 24 hour Museum portal website.

Nature And Countryside

Royal Society for the Protection of Birds (RSPB)

🖂 *The Lodge, Sandy, Bedfordshire, SG19 2DL*

☎ *01767 681577*

✎ *www.rspb.org.uk*

The largest wildlife conservation charity in Europe which owns or manages over 150 nature reserves covering more than 100,000 hectares.

Council for Protection for Rural England

⌨ *Warwick House,*
 25 Buckingham Palace Road, London, SW1W 0PP

☎ *020 7976 6433*

✐ *www.cpre.org.uk*

National charity which helps to protect, enhance and keep the countryside.

Countryside Agency

⌨ *John Dower House, Crescent Place,*
 Cheltenham, Gloucestershire, GL50 3RA

☎ *01242 521381*

✐ *www.countryside.gov.uk*

Responsible for advising government and taking action on issues affecting the social, economic and environmental well-being of the English countryside.

English Nature

⌨ *Northminster House,*
 Peterborough, Cambridgeshire, PE1 1UA

☎ *01733 455190*

✐ *www.english-nature.org.uk*

Responsible for 200 national nature reserves. They also organise a programme of walks and events.

Environment Agency

⌨ *Rio House, Waterside Drive,*
 Aztec West, Bristol, BS32 4UD

☎ *01454 624400*

✐ *www.environment-agency.gov.uk*

Wide ranging responsibilities and strong powers to protect and improve the environment.

Photography Credits

All photographs credited to Malcolm Briggs except the following.

p.8 'Beatles Story' courtesy of NorthWest Tourist Board / p.15 'Beadnell Bay' courtesy of Northumbria Tourist Board / p.33 courtesy of British Waterways Photolibary / p.37 courtesy of Northumbria Tourist Board / p.41 'La'al Rathy' courtesy of Cumbria Tourist Board / p.43 courtesy of British Waterways Photolibary / p.48 courtesy of Padstow Seafood School / p.51 © Andrew Kershman / p.59 courtesy of London Tourist Board / p.68 © Chris Windsor / p.71 'Flower Stall, Kendall Market' courtesy of Cumbria Tourist Board / p.75 © Andrew Kershman / p.87 'Hound Trailing' courtesy of Cumbria Tourist Board / p.91 © MCC / p.100 'Canoeing at Bednell' courtesy of Northumbria Tourist Board / p.106 courtesy of Canary Wharf Group / p.127 courtesy of Canary Wharf Group / p.131 ' Morris Dancers at Kirkby Stephen' courtesy of Cumbria Tourist Board / p.135 'Appleby Horse Fair' courtesy of Cumbria Tourist Board / p.141 courtesy of Canary Wharf Group / p.142 'Bamburgh Dusk' courtesy of Northumbria Tourist Board / p.145 courtesy of Geffrye Museum / p.148 courtesy of Victoria and Albert Museum / p.155 'Rheged Battle Re-enactment' courtesy of Cumbria Tourist Board / p.159 © Andrew Kershman / p.161 Shakespeare's Globe © Donald Cooper / 162 'Borough market' © Chris Windsor / p.164 courtesy of Hampton Court Palace